# Everything You Want to Know About How to Settle an Estate

# Everything You Want to Know About
# How to Settle an Estate

STEPHEN C. BRECHT

HASTINGS HOUSE
*Book Publishers*

Library of Congress Catalog Card Number 95-082025

ISBN 0-8038-9377-9

Text design by Irving Perkins Associates
Cover design © by Thomas Tafuri

Distributed by Publishers Group West
Emeryville, California

Printed in the United States of America

10  9  8  7  6  5  4  3  2  1

This book is dedicated with love to
my wife, Sara,
my children: Virginia, George, Edward, and Johnathan,
and my father, Franklin Ashley Brecht

# Special Thanks

I want to thank my publisher, Hy Steirman.

Because of his support for this book, thousands of individuals and their families across the country will have a clearer understanding of the probate process and retain more control over any estate settlement with which they are involved.

# Disclaimer

*How to Settle an Estate* explains the procedures of estate settlement and is intended to simplify these procedures while educating the reader.

It is neither a substitute for, nor an attempt to provide, legal advice. The author, publisher, their agents and assignees are not engaged in rendering legal, accounting, or other professional services or advice.

Though every attempt has been made to provide current and up-to-date information, the information should be checked with a professional against the most recent changes and developments. Neither the author, publisher, nor their agents and assignees can be held accountable for any error or omission contained herein, or in any other associated materials.

All individuals, families, and documents in the book are fictitious and are used for example purposes only. Any resemblance of individuals, families, or documents used in this book to real individuals, living or dead, families, or actual documents is purely coincidental.

# Contents

xi

# Everything You Want
## to Know About
# How to Settle
# an Estate

# The Phone Call

John Hook had known for several months that his father was terminally ill. The doctors held out little hope and had sent the elder Mr. Hook home from the hospital. John had flown from his home in Oregon to visit his father in Chicago when the diagnosis was made. It was during this visit that Mr. Hook told his son about his living trust document stored in the safe deposit at the local bank. He reminded John that he was named the successor trustee and that his responsibility was see that his two brothers and sister were taken care of after he was gone.

The fateful phone call came at 5:00 A.M. Pacific time when John's younger brother in Chicago told him that their father had passed away. John booked the first flight that day to Chicago. As the plane lifted off from Portland International Airport, John stared blankly out the window, his mind filled with memories of his father. He gave little thought to his new responsibilities.

# The Logical Choice

After Greg Goodwin returned from Korea, he married his childhood sweetheart, Mary, and settled down in Saint Joseph, Michigan. They bought a dry cleaning business, saved for a home, and started a family. They had enjoyed each other's company ever since they were teenagers. This didn't change as adults; they were best friends, a matched set. They worked together, built the business together, but they never dreamed they would die together. Their deaths were caused by a drunk driver who crossed the center line and struck Greg and Mary's car head-on. Their adult children were devastated by the tragedy.

One week after the funeral, the eldest daughter, Carolyn, while cleaning the house, found her parents' last will and testaments at the bottom of a desk drawer. They had been drawn up thirty-five years earlier when the kids were little. Husband and wife named each other as executor.

Unsure of what to do, she called a family meeting. It was agreed that she was the logical choice to take charge of clearing up Mom's and Dad's affairs.

# What If . . . ?

What if your spouse, parents, or someone else you knew passed away and named you in their will or trust? Or had asked you verbally to "take care of things" after they were gone? What if you received a letter from the probate court requesting you to wrap up the decedent's affairs?

What to do?

Where to begin?

You have to do something, but what?

The loss of a loved one is never easy. This is a trying time. To add to the emotional burden you are already carrying, in all likelihood, you are obligated to do something you have never done before—to navigate through the legal/emotional reefs of an estate settlement.

If you are named personal representative or executor of a will or successor trustee of a trust, don't despair. Help is at hand.

In all things remember: "Inch by inch life is a cinch, yard by yard it's very hard."

If you are named an heir, devisee, or beneficiary of an estate, what are your responsibilities? Certainly, you'd like to understand and follow the settlement process. How can you judge if things are being properly taken care of? When should you expect your inheritance?

# How to Use This Book

This book is specifically designed to guide you through an estate settlement.

1. If you are named as *personal representative, executor,* or *executrix* in a last will and testament, or appointed *administrator* by the probate court, use this book to understand what your exact responsibilities are as you navigate through the probate system. Remember to be patient.

2. If you are the original *trustee,* or have been named a *successor trustee* under a trust, use the information to

3

understand what powers you have at your disposal to settle an estate without a probate.

3. If you are named a *beneficiary* or *heir* in a last will and testament or trust, it will help to follow the process, keep up with the proceedings, or, if necessary, get another opinion as to what is taking place. Use this book as a benchmark against which the proceedings can be measured.

4. If you want an *attorney* to represent the estate before the court, use this book as a checklist with which to measure a legal representative. Become familiar with the legal language attorneys use. The law is a language in and of itself. Lawyers, like doctors, tend to speak in terms they know well, with little concern for the rest of us in our nonlegal, day-to-day lives.

Before hiring an attorney, use this book to prepare questions for your interview. In your selection process, do yourself a favor and become an informed consumer—ask A LOT of questions of the potential attorney "employee." That is exactly what he/she will be—your employee. The attorney is being hired to do a specific job.

# Some Thoughts About Attorneys, Wills, and Client Control

Some estate attorneys draw up a will for a small fee knowing it will be found later in the decedent's files or safe deposit box. The executor, executrix, or personal representative named in that document will, in all likelihood, contact that attorney who drew up this will for advice on how to proceed. Often, the attorney's reply is: "Don't worry, I'll handle everything."

He will, but agree on a price first.

The probate department of a legal firm generates a substantial amount of income. In fact, many lawyers look upon wills as a type of annuity. File cabinets filled with last will and testaments are sources of enormous future income.

Like most doctors, attorneys specialize in such areas as divorce, corporate law, marine law, international law, union negotiations, trial work, criminal law, civil law, etc. So not every attorney is schooled in representing an estate for the purpose of settling it. However, there are attorneys who specialize in estate settlement, probate, and the legal issues they involve.

Many people are intimidated by attorneys, especially those who have had little or no professional contact with them. How do you go about hiring an attorney? Don't be timid about discussing fees. Do you want the attorney to handle the whole estate or just part? Is it a flat rate, or an hourly charge? What about the quality of their services? What about extra charges? If the attorney handles the whole estate, be aware that attorneys may charge above and beyond what the court sets as a minimum. Ask about that before you make a decision.

Whether or not they deserve it, some people think of attorneys as opportunists, that somehow the attorney may take total control of the estate and its assets, and "legally" steal it. This happens very rarely. Recently, in California, an attorney was prosecuted for writing himself in for millions of dollars as an heir and beneficiary to the wills and trusts he was drawing up for his clients. He had been doing this for years! More and more states are passing laws to prevent attorneys from being named as heirs and beneficiaries in the last will and testaments or trusts they prepare for their clients.

You are under *no obligation* to retain the law firm or attorney who drew up the last will and testament to represent you in any legal proceeding. You are free to choose to use that attorney, a different attorney, or no attorney.

Before hiring an attorney, write out the questions that concern you. Here are some you should consider.

1. How long have you been practicing law?
2. How long has your firm been in business?
3. Is your practice confined to estates?
4. How many estates have you represented?
5. Are you representing any right now?
6. Can you estimate how long it will take to probate this estate (based on the following assets, number of creditors, and debts)?
7. Will you give me the names of three satisfied probate clients?

8. If you are allowed to charge "reasonable fees," please define "reasonable" and give me a written estimate.
9. Will you work with me on a "pro per" (as needed) basis?
10. Can I hire you to perform only specific parts of the probate?
11. Will you act as a "consultant" on those probate items I prefer to do myself?
12. Will you work on an hourly basis, in lieu of fees allowed by the court?
13. Will you sign a contract based on performance and timeliness?
14. Will you set a cap or limit on your fees?
15. Will you be prepared to stipulate a flat fee for *all* your services associated with probating this estate?
16. Will you sign an agreement to that effect?

Asking questions beforehand will save you much aggravation and time, and save the estate money in unnecessary legal fees. Do not be intimidated. An educated consumer has the power of choice and control.

# Other Resources

This book contains graphics, charts, and appendices to help you "see the big picture" that are designed to provide easy-to-read, at-a-glance information.

They are:

# What Is an Estate?

Simply put, it's *everything* of value that the deceased person owns at the time of death. It consists of all personal property, automobiles, boats, planes, motor homes, furniture, appliances, art, stamps and coins, dishes, and even clothes. It consists of any real estate that the decedent might have owned, including the home, any investment properties, commercial properties, vacant land, even vacation time-shares.

An estate also includes cash accounts, such as checking, savings, money market funds, CDs, treasury notes, retirement accounts, annuities, and life insurance policies. It is also made up of any stocks, bonds, mutual funds, secured notes, trust deeds (mortgages), partnerships, outstanding loans, and any business agreements. It is everything a person acquired during his or her lifetime and owned at the time of their passing. All of these items make up an "estate."

# What Is Estate Settlement?

Many people think that estate settlement deals only with how the assets, acquired over one's lifetime (and that of his/her spouse), should be distributed after their passing. But that is not the full picture of estate settlement.

Just as important as the distribution of assets to the heirs is the *management* of the decedent's estate while it is being settled. This management centers around closing bank accounts, selling assets, paying debts and taxes, keeping a property maintained or a business going, accounting for all of the assets in the estate, allocating assets or estate shares to the heirs, distributing assets to the heirs, making special bequests and gifts, seeing to the care of pets, and wrapping up the financial loose ends of a person's life.

To build up an estate, the average American will work approximately eighty-six thousand hours during a lifetime, the equivalent of forty years of full-time work. It is no wonder that estate settlement is a tricky, tedious, and demanding process.

# Where There's a Will (a Trust, or Even No Will), There's a Way

For the vast majority of us, an estate will be settled in one of five basic ways, or in some combination of these five. This is dictated by the type and kind of the assets in the estate, the level of valuation of the estate, the level and degree of estate planning accomplished before the passing of the individual, and the nature and relationship of the heirs or beneficiaries to the decedent.

These are the five basic ways to settle an estate.

1. By joint ownership of property, and ownership with right of survivor.
2. By designated beneficiary.
3. By the laws of intestate succession (no will).
4. By last will and testament.
5. By a trust.

Let's examine each one. . . .

# I. Estate Settlement by Joint Ownership of Property, Ownership with Right of Survivor

Consider the following situations in which the settlement of an estate would be simple. There would be no lengthy settlement process, no trust or last will and testament would be required, and legal intervention would, in many estates, be avoided.

## THE "EITHER/OR" ACCOUNT

Mr. and Mrs. Hoover are an elderly couple and residents of California. They do not own real estate, stocks, life insurance, or other investments. They have a jointly owned checking account of a little over $155,000. Their material needs are few.

Upon the passing of Mr. Hoover, his wife continues control of their one asset, the checking account. She can make deposits, write checks, and even spend the account to a zero balance.

That is exactly what Mrs. Hoover did. She spent all the funds during the ensuing years and passed away as a ward of the state of California.

The Hoovers' settlement procedure was very simple and straightforward. It was accomplished quickly and quietly on both the passing of husband and wife because:

1. They jointly owned and controlled their one asset, the checking account. This account was set up as an "either/or" account in which either spouse could access the account, sign checks, and spend the funds as they saw fit. Only one signature was needed. If this account had been set up as an "and" account, both signatures would have been needed to sign checks. At the passing of the first spouse, this would have put the estate in jeopardy of legal intervention.

This "either/or" technique of asset ownership provided the surviving spouse, Mrs. Hoover, access to the bank account and thus avoided legal hassles and delays.

2. When Mrs. Hoover passed away destitute, California made no claim, as there was nothing left in the Hoover estate to repay the government for the care it provided her.

# Joint Tenant Ownership Estates (Right of Survivor)

What about joint tenancy laws? If the decedent held an asset or other property as a joint tenant (a form of partnership) with another person, how will that estate be settled? The types of assets that can be held as joint tenants are real estate, stocks, bonds, partnership interests, and time-shares.

Under joint tenancy laws, when one person passes away, those assets held in joint tenancy will pass to the surviving joint tenant(s) automatically. This is because the surviving joint tenant(s) has a *right of survivor* to the decedent's share of that particular asset. This holds true no matter what relationship the joint tenants have to one another, or the number of joint tenants. The asset will simply transfer to the surviving joint tenant(s) without any delay.

If, for example, Mr. and Mrs. Edgington own their home as joint tenants with each other, there will be no question as to who will inherit the home when the first spouse passes away. The surviving spouse, either Mr. or Mrs. Edgington, will become the sole owner of that home because he/she is the only remaining joint tenant and has a right of survivor. That spouse may then file an affidavit of death of joint tenant with the county recorder or clerk to remove the name of the deceased joint tenant (spouse) from the deed to that home.

Sounds simple enough. However, caution is the rule of the day when title is held in joint tenancy:

1. Joint tenancy does not fully benefit the estate of the surviving joint tenant when another joint tenant dies. In reality, joint tenant ownership merely *defers* legal issues until the death of the surviving joint tenant. At that time, all those assets will be handled in a completely different manner, almost assuredly through the state probate court legal system.

2. Joint tenant ownership takes preference over the beneficiary in a last will and testament as to who inherits that particular asset. For example, what if the decedent owned a property as joint tenant with his or her friend John, but the last will and testament names his/her brother Edward as the heir for that asset? What will happen? John receives that share of the property when the decedent passes away. Poor brother Edward

will have no claim on "his" share. He was inadvertently disinherited because of joint tenancy laws.

3. Any other joint tenant "partner" can end or break the joint tenancy by selling his or her share. One could end up owning an asset with a "partner" not personally selected. This could result in undue stress in the relationship that might compel the surviving joint tenant to "dump" their share of the ownership. This could happen during a down market. Or the new "partner" may make the relationship very difficult, thus forcing a sale. It's quite common for someone to be forced out of an investment because of an unscrupulous "partner," or, worse, an unthinking spouse, parent, or friend.

4. The creditors of one joint tenant may attach his/her share, thereby negatively impacting the whole asset held in joint tenancy. If this happens, a court of law may order a partition action, a "forced sale," of that asset (usually at a distressed price) to satisfy the creditor's judgment. This happens frequently. In one case, a widow put her home in joint tenancy with her son to avoid probate, only to have the home sold from underneath her because of a judgment against the son due to a business failure. It's sad when something like this happens, but that's the law.

We are a nation of laws, not of justice, and there is a big difference between the two.

5. In some instances, a joint tenancy may inadvertently create a taxable gift to the partner. For example: Mr. George Early, a widower, transfers his home into joint tenancy with his daughter in an attempt to avoid probate when he passes away. He isn't aware that he has made a "gift" of one-half of the value of that property. If the value of this "gift" exceeds $10,000, Uncle Sam may be knocking on Mr. Early's door demanding a

37 percent gift tax on the value exceeding $10,000 (currently a parent may gift $10,000 to each child, once a year, tax free). Mr. Early may have to sell assets to pay those taxes. Gift taxes do not apply to joint tenancy transfers between husband and wife.

6. If the joint tenant becomes incapacitated due to an accident or medical condition, it may create difficulties. For example, if the property must be sold to generate cash to pay expenses, who will sign on behalf of the incapacitated joint tenant? If this person has not previously designated a conservator and/or attorney-in-fact, then the probate court will designate one. In either case, it will require full consent of the designee to complete the sale. Valuable time may be lost while awaiting consent. What happens if the designee doesn't agree to a sale? The estate may become obliged to start renegotiating, or give up valuable control of the asset.

7. There are also some very negative aspects of joint tenant ownership that relate to the paying of unnecessary income taxes on the sale of capital assets. "Capital assets" include real estate, stocks, coins, etc. For the purposes of this illustration, let's use a private home purchased a number of years ago for $50,000. That $50,000 becomes the *cost basis* of the property. Assume that in today's real estate market, the home has a *market value* of $200,000 (market value being the price you could expect to receive for this property).

The difference between the *cost basis* and the *market value* is called a *capital gain*, which, in our example, amounts to $150,000 in appreciation on that home. To put it bluntly, the government considers this a "profit" on that home, so it's subject to capital gains tax.

$$
\begin{array}{lll}
\text{Market value} & = & \$200,000 \\
\text{Cost basis} & = & \underline{\phantom{xx}50,000} \\
\text{Capital gain} & = & \$150,000
\end{array}
$$

How joint tenant ownership affects that capital gain can be very taxing. If a married couple held title to this home as joint tenants, the IRS has a surprise for the surviving spouse when the first spouse passes away.

For income tax purposes, Uncle Sam divides the home right down the center. They can do this because joint tenant ownership is nothing more than "equal ownership" under the law. One does not own a "whole" home valued at $200,000, only one-half, and the other spouse owns the second half. The original cost basis gets halved, so the husband's half is $25,000 and the wife's half is $25,000.

**COST BASIS**
*$50,000*

**$25,000    $25,000**
**Husband    Wife**

**MARKET VALUE**
*$200,000*

*$75,000*    *$75,000*
*"Profits"*  **Husband    Wife**

When the first spouse dies, the serious tax implications of holding title as joint tenants become evident. Upon the death of the first, one-half of the property will receive a special tax break called stepped-up valuation or stepped-up basis—it's the same. This means that his/

her original cost basis will be "stepped up" to the market value of his/her half as of the date of that spouse's passing.

Original or "old" cost basis    = $25,000
Stepped-up or "new" cost basis = $100,000

This tax break is not given to the surviving spouse. He/she does not qualify because this tax break is given at death only and the surviving spouse is still alive.

As the surviving joint tenant, the spouse receives the decedent's half of the home outside of probate by right of survivor. Together with the half he/she owns, the surviving spouse is now sole owner of a home valued at $200,000.

In addition, the surviving spouse would also "inherit" the deceased spouse's new stepped-up cost basis. Combining the deceased spouse's "new" cost basis and surviving spouse's "old" cost basis, the "adjusted" cost basis is $125,000.

Deceased spouse's "new" cost basis =   $100,000
Surviving spouse's "old" cost basis = + $25,000
Adjusted cost basis              =   $125,000

Assume the house is now too large, filled with too many memories, so the surviving spouse sells it for $200,000. The IRS will deduct the new adjusted cost basis from the sales price. The result will show a capital gain of $75,000.

Sales price          =    $200,000
Adjusted cost basis = − $125,000
Capital gain       =   $   75,000

However, the $75,000 "profit" may be taxed as ordinary income in the year it was received. Looking at a current 1996 federal income tax rate of 39 percent, and applicable state income tax, which, for example, is as high as 21 percent in New York, it could amount to a 60 percent tax bite.

These are dollars lost because of poor estate planning.

Now, let's take the same home, but this time it's titled as commonly owned property, sole and separate ownership, or in some states "community" property ownership. Under common, community property, or sole property ownership, the IRS can no longer come in and divide this home in half. This is because this property has "common" ownership and sole property is singular ownership. The ownership of the home is one unit and cannot be divided. If married, each spouse owns 100 percent of the home, all $200,000 worth. They also share the original cost basis of $50,000.

Upon the passing of the first spouse, the original cost basis of $50,000 gets "stepped up" to the full $200,000. If the surviving spouse sells the home, the tax liability will be strikingly different. The same holds true for sole ownership of property, where property is owned by only one individual.

| | | |
|---|---|---|
| Sales price | = | $200,000 |
| Stepped-up or "new" cost basis | = | −$200,000 |
| Taxable capital gain | = | -0- |

Since there is no "capital gain," there are no income or capital gain taxes due. By holding title to the home in community property, commonly owned property, or sole and separate property, all income tax liability was eliminated upon the sale of that asset.

The surviving spouse became almost $31,000 richer.

What if the surviving spouse chooses not to sell the property, and continues to live there? If he/she subsequently passes away owning that home, the surviving family will be able to transfer that property without legal intervention and obtain a second full stepped-up cost basis with all the tax benefits on the sale of capital assets. The heirs or beneficiaries will receive the property from the estate federal income tax (capital gain) free. However, the estate will not be "home free" because these forms of ownership are subject to probate. Even though there may be no income taxes, there will be heavy legal fees to be paid.

# 2. Estate Settlement by Designated Beneficiary

There is a type of asset that has an individual or individuals designated or named as beneficiary of it. A good example of this is life insurance. As long as the named beneficiary is not your estate, it will pass to that named beneficiary automatically. Other designated beneficiary assets include annuity contracts and retirement plans that are payable to a surviving spouse or named beneficiary.

This, however, does not apply to a last will and testament that names "beneficiaries" of the estate.

## LIFE INSURANCE

Mr. Robert Webb owns an insurance policy naming his wife as the beneficiary. Upon the passing of her husband, Mrs. Webb files a claim on this $150,000 life insurance policy.

Because life insurance, having a designated beneficiary, does not come under probate court jurisdiction. Mrs. Webb, as beneficiary of her husband's policy, avoided any and all legal processes. She simply filed a claim for the death benefit when she provided a certified copy of Mr. Webb's death certificate to the insurance carrier, and her claim was paid.

If, however, Mr. Webb had named "the estate of Robert Webb" as his beneficiary, then that asset would *not* have passed to Mrs. Webb without further legal implications upon the passing of her husband.

## OTHER ITEMS THAT WILL PASS AUTOMATICALLY

The following items pass to the heirs automatically, without additional legal requirements for passage, because of their nature:

1. Assets gifted away outright to another individual or to a trust during the decedent's lifetime.
2. Interests in trusts that terminate upon the passing of the beneficiary.
3. Property held in a trust. This will be discussed in more detail in the "Estate Settlement by Trust" section of this book
4. Bank accounts held "in trust for." These accounts are referred to as Totten trusts. A word of caution

regarding this type of account. Although this kind of trust account *should* pass automatically, nevertheless, some banks request an "order from a judge" to release funds held in this manner. The term "order from a judge" is a code phrase that means potential costly legal intervention.

5. Life-estate rights that terminate upon the death of the holder of the life estate.

# 3. Estate Settlement by Laws of Intestate Succession

What if the decedent owned assets that could not be distributed automatically and did nothing, *absolutely nothing at all*, to provide for that distribution or transfer upon his or her passing? This is the technique used by almost 70 percent of all Americans to distribute their estates. People use this technique for several reasons:

1. They feel immortal. There will be no need to distribute their estates. That may sound foolish, but it's amazing to hear so many people deny their mortality with *"That won't happen to me."*

2. They're too busy, or having too much fun, to take time to prepare the most basic estate planning. *"I've a good umpteen years before I need to think about that,"* they say, believing, if you don't think about it, it won't happen. In the vast majority of cases, death comes as a surprise. It's sad to know that with a few minutes of planning, they could have spared their loved ones a lot of grief, problems, and money.

3. Finally, there is the Rhett Butler philosophy. It goes like this: *"Frankly, my dear, I don't give a damn!"* Yes, there are folks who for one reason or another just don't care about what happens to those they leave behind—wives, children, or even aged parents.

If you make no plans and the inevitable happens, you will pass away *intestate*. Simply put, this means that a person who owned assets that could not be distributed automatically dies without leaving a last will and testament or heirs.

If this happened in your case, the probate court must decide who the heirs are and how they divide and share in the estate. Rarely does a distribution through intestacy match the distribution that the decedent would have made if he or she had made a last will and testament. They gave away control of their estate because they didn't care. Control is now vested with the court of competent jurisdiction in the decedent's state of residence *and* in any state where he or she owned non-probate-exempt property. The court's distribution plans are set by state law with little or no concern for the interests of the family. It benefits no one when someone dies intestate—not the family, the heirs, and not even the court system, which is usually overloaded and bogged down. The only ones who really benefit are the lawyers in the form of legal fees paid for carrying out the courts' choices.

## WHO WILL TAKE CHARGE?

If a full probate process is required, the court has the responsibility to name an "administrator." Where no full probate is required, the naming of an administrator will usually be waived.

Who is this administrator, and what does he or she do? The administrator is appointed by the court or surviving family members to be the estate representative. This person's job is the same as that of the personal representative, executor, or executrix named in a last will and testament. This person will manage the probate process and distribute the remainder of the assets to the heirs. There is specific rank ordering of who can be named administrator. The administrator must be a citizen or legal resident of the United States. To be named administrator, here is the order-of-priority selection process.

1. Surviving spouse. This person is first in line. However, if this surviving spouse was suing the decedent for support, divorce, or annulment, or is living separately from the decedent, his or her rank falls to level 7.
2. Children of the deceased. Usually, only one child is named. However, there can be "co-administrators" if more than one child wants, or demands through petition, to serve.
3. Grandchildren of the deceased.
4. Other downward bloodline issue of the deceased. These would include great-grandchildren.
5. Parents of the deceased.
6. Brothers and sisters of the deceased.
7. The issue (children) of the decedent's brothers and sisters, that is, nephews and nieces, the aunts, uncles, and first cousins of the deceased.
8. Grandparents of the deceased.
9. Issue (children) of the decedent's grandparents. These are the aunts, uncles and first cousins of the deceased.

10. The children of a predeceased spouse.
11. Other issue of a predeceased spouse. These would include the grandchildren of that predeceased spouse.
12. Others in the decedent's family line. This bloodline could become very thin, i.e., fourth cousin twice removed on the great-grandmother's side of the decedent's father!
13. The parents of the predeceased spouse.
14. Issue (children) of a predeceased spouse's grandparents. These are the aunts, uncles, and first cousins of the predeceased spouse.
15. Conservator or guardian of the estate of the deceased if appointed prior to the decedent's passing and legally acting as such in that capacity when the decedent passed away.
16. Public administrator appointed by the probate court.
17. Creditors of the decedent.
18. Any other interested party.

The processes of intestate succession are about the same in all fifty states, though each state has its own set of laws.

The laws of intestate succession also apply if all named heirs and beneficiaries in a last will and testament or trust and their issue (children) are deceased at the time of the distribution of the estate. Upon such occurrence, the estate would be distributed to living "upline" blood relatives and family members of the decedent such as parents, brothers, sisters, nieces, nephews, and so forth.

# Intestate Succession

Assets distribution if decedent is not survived by children or grandchildren.

PARENTS

IF NOT LIVING THEN →

BROTHER or SISTER

NIECE or NEPHEW

← IF NOT LIVING THEN

IF NOT LIVING THEN →

FIRST COUSIN

GREAT NIECE or GREAT NEPHEW

← IF NOT LIVING THEN

IF NOT LIVING THEN →

FIRST COUSIN Once Removed

SECOND COUSIN

← IF NOT LIVING THEN

# 4. Estate Settlement by Last Will and Testament

## WHAT IS A LAST WILL AND TESTAMENT AND WHAT DOES IT DO?

A last will and testament is nothing more than instructions to the probate court. That's the only function it has. It tells the probate court judge how the decedent wants his or her estate distributed to the beneficiaries. However, the probate court judge can throw out this last will and testament and substitute it with a court-imposed plan of distribution. The probate court is *not* bound by the distribution instructions in a will.

A last will and testament does not protect an estate from inheritance taxes or income taxes. It is not designed to accomplish these goals. In order to provide that protection, you need other estate planning tools.

A story that appeared in the nation's newspapers on November 1, 1995, startled the legal community when it was announced that the late Warren Burger, former Chief Justice of the United States, had prepared a sloppy will that might cost his heirs approximately $500,000.

After his wife's death in 1994, the Chief Justice typed up a one-page will on his computer. He bequeathed two-thirds of his $1,800,000 estate to his son, Wade, and one-third to his daughter, Margaret.

The former Chief Justice not only misspelled words but he did not grant executors the power to sell his real estate to pay taxes; this required special permission from the probate court. The result not only increased his attorneys' fees and court costs, but also increased his estate and federal taxes.

## WILL CHALLENGES AND OTHER CONSIDERATIONS

To provide for the distribution of an estate, there are several considerations to take into account when working with a typical last will and testament: control of distribution and fees and taxes charged against the estate.

The first consideration is that of control. The typical will can provide an estate with "control" as to how the assets may be distributed among the heirs, provided that the probate court agrees and the will is not challenged.

Unlike passing away intestate, wherein the court will determine who gets what and when, a last will and testament helps "control" the distribution of the decedent's estate. I have put the word "control" in quotation marks because the will may be wasted if the estate is challenged in the probate court by an unhappy heir. One-third of all last will and testaments are challenged by brothers and/or sisters after a parent passes away. A last will and testament is no guarantee that the decedent's wishes will be honored. The probate court will think nothing of throwing out his or her directions and superseding them with their own, or those of a third party.

Challenges to the will come in two forms—substantival and procedural. Both these forms of challenge can, if proved, be grounds for invalidating the decedent's last will and testament.

Substantival challenges are usually made if the

mental state of the decedent at the time that he or she signed the will is questioned. The term "being of sound mind" is almost a caricature phrase—everyone has heard it. What it means is that the signer of the will, called a testator if a male and testatrix if a female, understood the import and knew the names of all those to whom assets or property were to be distributed. We have all heard of "undue influence," wherein force or duress was used to influence the signer of the will. The concept of "undue influence" does not include mere personal persuasion.

The second form a challenge may take is procedural in its attack. This means that the will challenge is based on some mistake or flaw when it was written, executed, or witnessed. A good example of a procedural attack is when two last will and testaments outlining different distribution plans are presented to the court.

If the will is challenged on any grounds, the probate process will stop instantly. Any and all challenges must be cleared before the process can go forward and ultimately conclude. Challenges can be very messy and expensive, and an attorney is almost always needed to defend against them. Many lawyers will help challenge a will on a contingency fee basis. This means that the challenger does not have to pay a lawyer in advance and the lawyer receives a percentage of the inheritance as a fee. During probate, many frivolous challenges that halt the process are settled by the rightful heirs in order to get things moving. This is a drain on the estate assets, and is very frustrating.

A last will and testament does not reduce or avoid taxes or other fees that may be assessed against the decedent's estate. As stated earlier, a will is not designed to deal with those issues, it only ensures that the estate is probated.

# Probate—The Court-Controlled Process of Estate Settlement

Probate. What does it mean?

Why do the courts get involved in an estate after someone has passed away? Let me give you a simple definition. Probate means "to prove." Strictly speaking, in order to have a "probate," there must be a last will and testament, because what is being "proved" is the validity of that will. For our purposes, the term "probate" means the entire court process used to settle an estate that cannot be distributed legally in any other manner. Even if an individual passed away without a will (intestate), the nature of the assets in the estate could cause that estate to be brought under the jurisdiction of the probate court system.

Probate is the process by which the decedent's last will and testament is "proved" valid, his or her name is removed from a title or an asset, legal and financial matters are settled, creditors are paid, and, finally, the remainder of the estate's assets are distributed to the beneficiaries (heirs).

Thus, if one passes away possessing real estate, individually owned bank accounts, stocks or bonds as an individual owner, their name will have to be removed from all those assets before such assets can be transferred. But transferred by whom? The owner isn't here and can no longer sign over those assets to his or her heirs.

All fifty states have established a probate process whereby the state, through the courts, takes over control of the estate to make sure that all debts are paid, affairs are settled properly, and the assets transferred, hopefully in accordance with the decedent's wishes. If the estate should fall under the jurisdiction of the probate court, this court will have almost full and total control over that estate and all of its assets while the decedent's affairs are sorted out (see Appendix I).

# Types of Probate

There are four general categories of "probate": supervised, unsupervised, small estate (summary), and ancillary.

## SUPERVISED PROBATE

*Supervised* probate is the form most commonly thought of when the word "probate" is used. It can, depending on the state, be termed formal, regular, court-administered, even solemn. Supervised probate *requires* court oversight, approval and administration of *all* the steps needed to settle the estate. It can require the estate to use court-approved personnel.

Even an estate that doesn't require supervision may be brought under court control and oversight if the named personal representative, executor, executrix, or administrator is not perceived by the court or other interested parties to be capable of handling the estate. If an heir believes that his or her interests might not be met adequately, that person may request that the estate go through a supervised process.

## UNSUPERVISED PROBATE

*Unsupervised* probate involves less court supervision and qualifies because of the value of the estate, or distribution of the assets to the heirs. This probate process is also called informal, streamlined, common, independent, or short-form, depending on the state of jurisdiction.

Even if the last will and testament of the decedent authorizes the personal representative, executor, or executrix to use the unsupervised method, state law or other concerns could still force the estate into a supervised process. Just because the estate qualifies for an unsupervised process does not release the personal representative, executor, executrix, or administrator from successfully performing all those tasks required to settle the estate as detailed in the "Anatomy of a Probate" section farther on.

The main difference between supervised and unsupervised probate administration is the reporting processes required at each step. Both are "file and wait" processes; unsupervised probate is faster, as you do not have to wait for numerous open court dates or appointments with the judge or probate registrar.

A very big downside of unsupervised probate is the accountability factor. The personal representative, executor, executrix, or administrator is accountable to both the heirs and the creditors of the estate. If he or she does not perform the tasks exactly as prescribed by law, there could be additional legal implications. With supervised probate, the ball is always in the court's court, so to speak. Responsibility rests with the court, as does the accountability for the process and its outcome.

## SMALL ESTATE OR SUMMARY PROBATE

Small estate probate is also called summary, mini, affidavit, even "rubber stamp." It is by far the simplest, fastest, and easiest of all the probate processes.

Every state sets a level of valuation below which there is no need for a lengthy and cumbersome probate in order to pass the decedent's estate to his or her heirs. If, at the time of passing, the estate is inventoried and appraised at a value below the probate threshold in that state of residence, the heirs will inherit the estate free from probate. Property owned in a state other than that of residency requires appraisal of assets in that second state. If the established value falls below that state's valuation threshold, the estate will also avoid probate in that state as well.

Under these conditions, the personal representative, executor, executrix, or administrator should be able to file a petition with the court for summary probate. This is a simple process whereby an accounting and affidavit of worth are filed with the probate court. If there is no challenge or creditor claims made within the statutory time frame, the judge will "rubber stamp" the petition as accepted and this mini-probate will have been quickly, and simply, completed. At that point, the assets can be distributed to the heirs and the estate closed and settled.

A summary probate requires one to two months and costs several hundred dollars.

## ANCILLARY PROBATE

*Ancillary* probate comes into play when the decedent owned property in a different state than place of residency. Probate is a state-specific process. Even with the Uniform Probate Code, each state still has its own set of rules, regulations, and guidelines. Ancillary probate can be either supervised, unsupervised, or summary.

For example, let's look at the estate of Mrs. Andrew Linn, a widow. She owned a home in Upstate New York and a vacation condo on the Gulf Coast of Florida. When Mrs. Linn passed away, her executor had to file for probate in *both* New York *and* Florida. If the decedent had owned property in other states, probate would have had to be filed in those states as well.

If this second state is a long way from where the personal representative, executor, or executrix lives, it could cause great hardship and travel expense. Many states require a "resident agent" to be named to represent the estate in the state where the property is owned. Some states go so far as to require that a second personal representative, executor, executrix, or administrator be named who lives within the borders of that state. This is usually a local attorney or government employee.

# Anatomy of a Probate

The following is the legal estate settlement process that Greg and Mary Goodwin's daughter Carolyn faced after they were killed by the drunk driver. The Goodwins' probate will be supervised through the probate court in the county of their last residence under Michigan Statutes Annotated Ch. 27.5001-27.5993, Michigan Court Rules (Probate Court).

The administration of the Goodwin estate will use all areas of a supervised probate process. Of course, each probate is different, and the process in your particular situation may vary to a greater or lesser degree from that represented herein. The following is a diagram of the probate process. See chart on pages 36–37.

This is the journey Carolyn Goodwin is about to embark on.

# Step I. Locate and Read the Will

After making arrangements for funeral and burial, the first step in settling the decedent's estate is to locate the last will and testament. At this same time, you may also want to collect and forward, but not cancel, the decedent's mail. You should cancel magazine, newspaper, and other subscriptions. Place a number referral on the telephone. Cancel cable services, and all credit cards. Do *not* pay off the outstanding balances on these cards until you get a final or closing statement. Some companies, as a courtesy to the decedent's survivors, may forgo payment of the balance if it is small.

Notify the Social Security Administration and other federal, state, and local government agencies if they were providing benefits to the decedent. Follow their instructions as to the procedures they require for the return of checks, and termination benefits and services.

## HOW DO I KNOW A WILL EXISTS AND WHERE DO I LOOK FOR IT?

People consider their last will and testament to be an important legal document. Most take some trouble to protect it from loss, damage, or destruction. In my example, Carolyn found her parents' wills in a desk drawer at their home.

The decedent's home is a good place to start the search. Look in all drawers, filing cabinets, home safes, Bibles or other religious books, and between books in bookcases. Use your imagination. We had a client who kept his last will and testament in an airtight plastic bag in the freezer, under the rainbow trout! His reasoning was clear as to why he chose this location. "If there's a fire, it'll be protected from flames and water," he told me. While this would protect the will, it would also create problems. He could have passed away and his children would have had quite an adventure finding it.

Check other locations: See if the decedent has a bank safe deposit box (you may need a court order to open it); check the family lawyer, the county probate registrar, county clerk, his place of business, or the homes of friends or relatives.

A last will and testament can take several forms. It can be a fill-in-the-blank form from the stationery store or a "formal" will drafted by a lawyer, paralegal, estate planner, or computer program. It can be a handwritten (holographic) document of many pages or a

# Probate of the Goodwin Estate

**LOCATE & READ THE WILL**
Handle all funeral arrangements.

Meet with family members and other interested parties who might require information. If possible, consult with the attorney who drew up the Will(s) and any other people familiar with the decedent's affairs.

**SAFEGUARD ESTATE ASSETS**

Notify banks, safe deposit, and others.

Examine all books, accounts, and files.

Acquire knowledge of business interests.

Review insurance and protect all assets.

**PETITION THE COURT FOR PROBATE OF ESTATE**

**PUBLISH PUBLIC / CREDITOR NOTICES**

**ASSEMBLE AND INVENTORY ALL ESTATE ASSETS**

Review condition, leases, taxes, and mortgages on real estate. Manage same.

Gain custody of securities. Collect interest, dividends, and payments.

Arrange for supervision and management of on-going business.

Claim for $ due. Gain evidence & witnesses on contested claims.

Inventory and appraise personal property.

**OBTAIN APPRAISAL OF ALL ASSETS**
Value as of date of death (± 6 months).

Collect life insurance policies and cash. Secure tax waivers.

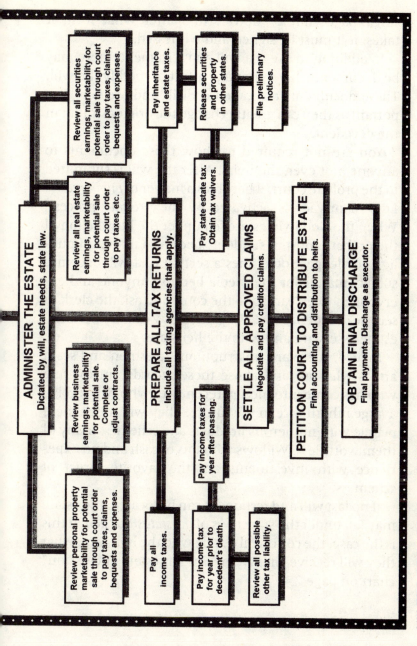

**ADMINISTER THE ESTATE**
Dictated by will, estate needs, state law.

Review all securities earnings, marketability for potential sale through court order to pay taxes, claims, bequests and expenses.

Pay inheritance and estate taxes.

Release securities and property in other states.

File preliminary notices.

Review all real estate earnings, marketability for potential sale through court order to pay taxes, etc.

Review business earnings, marketability for potential sale. Complete or adjust contracts.

Review personal property marketability for potential sale through court order to pay taxes, claims, bequests and expenses.

**PREPARE ALL TAX RETURNS**
Include all taxing agencies that apply.

Pay state estate tax. Obtain tax waivers.

Pay income taxes for year after passing.

Pay all income taxes.

Pay income tax for year prior to decedent's death.

Review all possible other tax liability.

**SETTLE ALL APPROVED CLAIMS**
Negotiate and pay creditor claims.

**PETITION COURT TO DISTRIBUTE ESTATE**
Final accounting and distribution to heirs.

**OBTAIN FINAL DISCHARGE**
Final payments. Discharge as executor.

single-page simple "note." No matter what form it takes, it it must be signed and witnessed.

In addition to the last will and testament, there may be documents that materially affect or modify the will. These documents are called codicils and are very important as they can greatly change the original intent of the decedent.

You are not required to show these documents to anyone, not even the heirs. After the will is submitted to the probate court, it becomes a matter of *public record*. Loss of privacy is activated by the probate process. When the Goodwin estate fell under the jurisdiction of the probate court, it suddenly became a matter of public knowledge. Sometimes a section of a will becomes subject matter for the media because anyone and everyone in town can go to the court and ask the clerk to see the decedent's file. They will know exactly what the estate assets are and who the heirs are.

Indeed, there are unscrupulous salesmen and scam artists who use and abuse these records, uncovering who has come into money recently or who will receive a large inheritance in the future. They will solicit these people with numerous products and schemes, many of them worthless. Widows with lots of cash and no experience with investments are the favorite target of schemers.

If no last will and testament can be located, the estate may fall under the state laws of *intestate succession*. If this is the case, the court will decide who the heirs are, what they will receive, and when. See "Intestate Succession" chart on page 25.

## READING THE WILL

Okay, you found the will in an old coffee can on the top shelf of the pantry. Make six to twelve copies of it for everyday use and secure the original in a safe place.

You have to present this signed (and witnessed) *original* document to the probate court. This will be covered later.

You may decide to read the will to the family, though this is not required. A typical last will and testament is centered on the decedent's final wishes and instructions for the distribution of his or her assets. It basically says, "Give this to him and that to her. I'm still thinking clearly, there's no threat to me, and I want this done my way."

The reading of the will is usually an informal affair. The family members gather to hear what the decedent had to say in his/her final remarks and what each will receive from the estate at the end of probate.

A new twist to reading the will has come about with the popularity of the home video camera and VCR. I have heard of instances where the family members are instructed to sit in a certain order in front of the television set. When the tape was played, the decedent was able to look each family member directly in the eye and tell him or her off!

You might want to consult with the lawyer who drew up the will for any insights he can provide you.

# Mary Goodwin's Will

The following is Mary Goodwin's last will and testament. Her husband Greg's will contains the same provisions and therefore is not shown here. This is the document her daughter Carolyn will submit to the probate court.

The following is an example of a typical, simple last will and testament, but is by no means the only form this type of document can take. It covers the basic provisions of a will in that it:

*1. Identifies the decedent.*

**Last Will and Testament
of
Mary I. Goodwin**

**I, Mary I. Goodwin, of Saint Joseph, Michigan, being of sound mind do hereby revoke any former Wills and Codicils and declare this to be my Last Will and Testament.**

*2. Provides for payment of debts and certain expenses.*

**Article I
Payment of Debts and Expenses**

**I direct that my just debts, funeral expenses, and expenses of last illness be first paid from my estate.**

*3. Names who is to receive assets from the estate.*

Article II
Disposition of Property

A. Specific Bequests. I direct that the following specific bequest be made from my estate. However, such bequest shall be made only if my spouse, Greg A. Goodwin, does not survive me.

1. Five hundred ($5,000.00) dollars shall be distributed to the City of Saint Joseph, Michigan, Animal Shelter.

B. Residuary Estate. I direct that my residuary estate be distributed to my spouse, Greg A. Goodwin. If my spouse does not survive me, my residuary estate shall be distributed to my children in equal shares. If a child of mine does not survive me and has no children who survive me, such deceased child's share shall be distributed in equal shares to my other children. If no child of mine survives me, and if none of my deceased children are survived by children, my residuary estate shall be distributed to the following organization:

The City of Saint Joseph Animal Shelter, 970 Colfax Avenue, Saint Joseph, Michigan.

*4. Names who is to handle her final affairs and settle the estate.*

### Article III
### Nomination of Executor

I nominate my husband, Greg A. Goodwin, of Saint Joseph, Michigan, as the Executor of my estate.

*5. Gives powers to the named executor.*

### Article IV
### Executor Powers

My Executor, in addition to other powers and authority granted by law or necessary or appropriate for proper administration, shall have the right and power to lease, sell, mortgage, or otherwise encumber any real or personal property that may be included in my estate.

*6. Identifies other parties to her last will and testament.*

### Article V
### Miscellaneous Provisions

A. Spouse. I am married to Greg A. Goodwin and all references in this Will to "my spouse" are references to Greg A. Goodwin.

C. Children. The names of my children are: Carolyn I. Goodwin, William R. Goodwin, Donna J. Goodwin, and Richard A. Goodwin. All references in this Will to "my children" include the above children.

*7. Is signed and witnessed.*

> IN WITNESS WHEREOF, I have subscribed my name below, this 14th day of October, 1956.
>
> ————————————————————————
>
> Mary I. Goodwin
>
> We, the undersigned, hereby certify that the above instrument was signed in our sight and presence by Mary I. Goodwin (the "Testatrix"), who declared this instrument to be her Last Will and Testament and we, at the Testatrix's request and in the Testatrix's sight and presence, and in the sight and presence of each other, do hereby subscribe our names and addresses as witnesses on the date shown above.
>
> Witness Signature: ————————————————
>
> Witness Name: George B. Cox
> Witness Address: 1066 Hastings Lane, Benton's Harbor, Michigan
>
> Witness Signature: ————————————————
>
> Witness Name: Carmen O. Cox
> Witness Address: 1066 Hastings Lane, Benton's Harbor, Michigan

At first review, Mary's last will and testament seems as if it would be very easy and simple to deal with. It is so short and understandable. However, as tends to be the case with most "thin" documents, there are problems with Mary's "simple" will document. This document is flawed. One flaw is obvious (can you find it?), the other hidden. These flaws can therefore cause confusion, mixed signals, and legal entanglements.

For instance, look at the following statement:

> C. Children. The names of my children are: Carolyn I. Goodwin, William R. Goodwin, Donna J. Goodwin, and Richard A. Goodwin. All references in this Will to "my children" include the above children.

This seems straightforward and to the point, so what's the problem? It just so happens that several years after Mary signed this will, Greg and Mary became the adoptive parents of an individual who is not named in her will. Was this an oversight on Mary's part or was it intentional? Is this adopted child one of the heirs to the estate? If so, in what portion?

Did you spot the other flaw?

> A. Specific Bequests. I direct that the following specific bequest be made from my estate. However, such bequest shall be made only if my spouse, Greg A. Goodwin, does not survive me.
> 1. Five hundred ($5,000.00) dollars shall be distributed to the City of Saint Joseph, Michigan, Animal Shelter.

Do you see it? If I were the director of the animal shelter I would hope to receive a check in the amount of *$5,000*. If I were Carolyn, I would hope Mom had *$500* in mind. Which is it?

Either of these flaws could cause a procedural challenge. If this will is challenged, the probate court will have the final say. This could be the cause of much confusion and expense to straighten it out.

In addition, look at the date of this will. It was signed in 1956. As of the publication date of this book, Mary Goodwin's last will and testament is forty years old. She had put it in the desk drawer and never updated, revised, or thought of it again. This will is "stale" and could be challenged on the grounds that it really did not reflect her desires and wishes at the time of her death.

# Step 2. Safeguarding Estate Assets

Locating and reading the will are very important estate settlement steps that are prerequisites for starting the probate. This is also true for safeguarding the estate assets.

Carolyn Goodwin has not yet started the official probate process. She is beginning a very steep learning curve and has to uncover or discover as much information as possible about her parents' affairs. In fact, she must find out *everything* concerning the financial, creditor, business, banking, investing, real estate, and all other asset-based information. She must take care not to overlook assets or lose track of them in this process. Being organized, patient, and having knowledge-collection skills are critical in this phase.

Speak with business experts and managers,

stockbrokers, financial advisers, or other people familiar with the decedent's affairs. Try to bring them up to speed as quickly as possible.

## GETTING ORGANIZED

A very important part of proper estate settlement is asset and document organization. You will need to have a very simple yet effective way of organizing the important documents and assets you uncover. It should be easy to work with and provide a "one-stop" system to find any and all needed documentation and information.

The best tool to accomplish this is to have an "estate settlement organizer." I have found that the most effective organizer is a three-ring loose-leaf binder. This binder should include section dividers, and have pockets on the inside front and back covers.

This organizing tool should contain the following documents and information:

1. Copies of the decedent's last will and testament or living trust and any codicils or trust amendments. All correspondence concerning his or her passing.
2. At least one *certified* copy of the death certificate. You probably received eight to twelve copies from the funeral home. If you need additional certified copies of the death certificate, you can go directly to the county clerk's office.
3. Any list or memorandum used to give small personal items, such as a family heirloom, to a named individual.
4. A directory of the phone numbers and mailing addresses of any and all people you want and need to notify of the passing.

5. A personal data profile that records the decedent's personal information, such as birth date and place, Social Security number, driver's license number, marriage date, the names of parents and children, and any other information you deem important to the process.
6. The decedent's durable power of attorney for asset management, if one exists.
7. The decedent's living will, right to die clause, or physicians' directive.
8. Guardianship papers for any minor children, or adult handicapped children.
9. A brief financial statement worksheet of the estate's estimated value. This will be updated as more information is discovered.
10. A savings and investment section containing voided photocopies of decedent's assets as follows:
    Checking accounts
    Savings accounts
    Credit union accounts
    Money market accounts
    Certificates of deposit
    Treasury bills
    Stock and bond certificates
    Mutual funds
    Notes receivable
    Tax-deferred retirement plans
    Profit-sharing plans
    Individual retirement accounts
    Keogh plans
    Tax-sheltered annuities
11. Copies of all real estate deeds, recorded and unrecorded, along with a property tax bill for each parcel.

12. The face page of all insurance policies.
13. Gift/loan accounting section.
14. Business agreements and documentation.
15. Any important business cards associated the decedent's affairs.

This is a preliminary estate settlement step not controlled by the probate court. What is done in this step will directly impact on the probate process. Remember that what you are doing here is preliminary in nature, "getting your ducks in a row" and organizing yourself. Probate is never easy, but without organization, it will feel impossible and overwhelming.

## LIKE BEES TO HONEY

Do you remember the film *Zorba the Greek*, starring Anthony Quinn as Zorba? I have always considered it an excellent motion picture. Not only in filmmaking and storytelling, but also its revealing of one of life's most poignant moments. In the film, there is a scene in which Zorba's "wife" dies. As she lies dying, the other women in the village are just waiting to swoop down like vultures. As soon as she passes away, they literally invade the house and begin to carry off everything she owned. Zorba tries frantically to stop them from taking all of his departed wife's clothes, furniture, and other personal effects. However, these women are just too numerous for Zorba to overcome. They take everything, even the sheets on the deathbed where she lies, leaving the house completely empty and Zorba totally defeated.

There is a life lesson in this scene from *Zorba*. That lesson is this: If one is not prepared, chaos will prevail.

Safeguarding the estate assets, and being organized, are critical to estate settlement and probate management.

# Review All Forms of Insurance and Protect All Assets

The decedent probably owned or carried several insurance policies. They would include some or all of the following.

## LIFE INSURANCE

Though insurance passes free of probate, you might want to wait before filing a claim. It could be too early to file a claim for death benefits. A large infusion of cash at this time could cause a negative taxable situation. You can always file a claim at a later date if you decide to wait.

It is a good idea to start assembling the policies and other documents needed to file the claim at the appropriate time. You need a certified copy of the decedent's death certificate and the name of the policy provider and policy number to make the claim. Look for policies in the same places you looked for the will. If you cannot find a policy but think that the decedent had one, try reviewing canceled checks for at least a year prior to the decedent's passing. If you find one made to and deposited by a company, talk to a local agent of that company.

He or she will be happy to help you. If there is no local agent, try directory assistance for the phone number of the main office in the city where the check was deposited.

Some credit card companies, banks, and other organizations provide their clients and members with life insurance, as do some employers. The premiums are not paid by the decedent, so no check record will be found.

## HEALTH INSURANCE

Cancel this policy if there is no legal action filed or pending and if it is not a joint plan with a surviving spouse for example. Make sure to ask for a refund of the unused portion of the coverage period—you may just get one. If you are unsure about canceling this policy, consult with legal counsel before you take any action that could in any way compromise its benefit to the estate.

## VEHICLE INSURANCE

If a motor vehicle of any type, boat, or plane is part of the estate, you should not cancel the corresponding insurance policies right now. These assets will still need to be protected as long as they are in the estate.

## HOMEOWNER'S OR RENTER'S INSURANCE

If the decedent's residence is comprised of real property, you should not cancel the homeowner's policy. This asset will still need to be protected as long as it is in the estate. The same is true for insurance on all other real property that was owned by the decedent.

If the decedent did not own a home but instead rented a house, condominium, or apartment, do not cancel any renter's coverage on personal property until such time as *all* of the personal property is safely removed from the residence. Again, if you are unsure about canceling this policy, consult with legal counsel before you take any action.

## BUSINESS INSURANCE AND PROFESSIONAL PRACTICE INSURANCE (ERRORS AND OMISSIONS)

Many businesses are also insurable. Business insurance is a lot like homeowner's insurance. It pays the business in the event of inventory loss due to fire, flood, theft, or other situation. It protects the business in the event the business is sued by an injured party. Insurance papers for the business will probably be located at the business site. There may be a certificate of insurance provided by the carrier.

Professional practitioners such as doctors, lawyers, real estate brokers and stockbrokers, and accountants, to name a few, can have a special type of insurance wherein they are protected in the event they are sued by an injured party for something that the decedent did, or did not do (omission).

If the business is still running and will in all probability continue until the court decides what to do, you will want to keep the insurance active. Consult the writing agent if you have any questions.

# Acquire Knowledge of Business Interests

A second piece of the safeguarding puzzle is to acquire information about the decedent's employment and/or business interests. If the decedent was an employee, contact the employee benefits department or personnel office where he/she worked. Obtain the deceased employee's last paycheck. Even if the employee did not die on the job or as a result of it, there may be additional benefits provided by the employer such as insurance, severance pay, vacation pay, survivors' assistance, etc. Make sure you ask about these and other supplemental benefits or payments.

If the decedent owned a business, it was conducted as one of the following forms: sole proprietor, partnership, or corporation. These are the three forms all businesses will take. Whichever form it takes, it will be a challenge to "get up to speed" on the decedent's interest in that business.

If the decedent ran the business as a sole proprietorship, it is possible that the business will die along with its owner, unless there is someone to step in and pick up the torch. Even if no one steps forward, you can't just close and lock the door. If you can't find a buyer, you must be prepared to systematically close the business. This includes letting the employees go and providing their last paychecks, paying off the suppliers and creditors, negotiating and paying the final rent, disposing of inventory, stock, and fixtures, settling any customer claims, providing refunds on work not completed, and/or selling either a portion of the business or all of it, lock, stock, and barrel.

If the business is a partnership in which one or more of the partners are still living and active in its day-to-day running, or if it is a corporation, it will probably remain in operation. In this case, the business has not died. Partnerships and corporations are "entities" in and of themselves. You can think of them like a paper person, and, as such, they don't die of natural causes as we do, they must be terminated legally.

You might also want to consult with business advisers and managers or other people familiar with the decedent's business affairs. Try to bring them up to speed as quickly as possible. Probate is never an enabling framework within which to maintain an ongoing business venture. There is little one can do, under a supervised process, that does not need to be approved and blessed by the court in some manner. It is a time-consuming and bureaucratic process. Having competent "advisers" at your disposal can make a bad situation somewhat more tolerable.

# Notify Banks, Safe Deposits, and Other Interested Parties

This portion of the settlement process, though time-consuming, is the notification to interested parties. Inform all financial institutions where the decedent did business or had an account that he/she has passed away. This would include: banks (domestic and foreign), brokerage houses, safe deposit accounts, trust companies, investment firms, savings and loan organizations, credit unions, private lenders, and mortgage or trust deed holders.

It's extremely important to notify all these companies to avoid the possibility of fraud. It's amazing how many times accounts have been drained of funds and closed by people impersonating the deceased (including unauthorized check-cashing). In addition, these companies have to be informed that the estate is soon to be brought into the probate court. This helps you because the sooner these companies complete their paperwork for you, the sooner you can move on to the next probate step.

You will not be closing any accounts at this time, that will come later. This step merely puts these firms on notice that a death has occurred.

How do you uncover where the decedent had his/her accounts? Look in three places: the first place is in the decedent's files and papers. Hopefully, your search will start and end there. If not, the second place is the decedent's checkbook(s). Put together a record of all checks for at least one year. It may be that the decedent's accountant has the canceled checks to complete tax forms. The third place to look is at the mail. You can't notify a company until you can find out the name of the company. Conversely, the company won't know the client passed away until you tell them. This will stop them from needlessly sending bills and statements other than final accounting.

If the decedent owes money, each creditor must file a claim through the court process. Don't worry about paying decedent's debts. The court will supervise that.

# Examine All Books, Accounts, and Files

Aside from notifying these companies, review *all* the decedent's papers and files. Banks read the obituaries and, in some states, will "freeze" accounts and the safe deposit box so no one has access except under court supervision.

Index the files into two broad groups, personal papers and financial/asset papers. Be on the lookout for real estate deeds. If you know that the decedent owned property but you can't find the deeds, it is easy to get copies. Call the property tax assessor's office. Give them the address of the property. They will tell you who the owner is and the property tax identification number that is sometimes called the assessor's parcel number (APN). With this APN number, you can now get a copy of the deed from the county recorder's office. Make sure that it is a certified or officially recognized copy.

Don't throw anything away. What a paper looks like may not necessarily be what it is, and you might be sorry later. Let the following true story be a lessen. Several years ago, after the passing of an elderly gentleman, a member of the family was getting rid of "junk," including a dusty old shoe box from the garage of his home. "Just ol' letters and junk," she told her brother as she pitched it into the trash. He didn't think much about it, assuming that his sister had reviewed the letters. But two days later, he started to think about those old letters sitting out there in the trash.

He tried to ignore them, but by the third evening,

they were nagging at him. After dinner, he drove to the decedent's house, went through the trash can, and retrieved that old, dusty, unmarked shoe box. Inside he found about a dozen letters written in old-fashioned penmanship, signed by a man named Sam—Samuel Langhorne Clemens, known to the entire world as Mark Twain! What you at first consider junk could, at second look, be valuable. Maybe not on the scale as the above story, but still important. Even if it has no dollar value, like an old family photo, it might still have a lot of personal value to a family member.

What may have had value in one form and lost that value may have a different value now. A good example of this are old stock certificates of failed companies. They have no value in shares but are very collectible.

When in doubt, call an expert or spend a little time at the library researching that potential treasure trove discovered in a box at the bottom of the file cabinet or out in the garage.

## Are You Ready?

So far, things have been very informal. Carolyn has located and read her parents' last will and testaments and consulted with other people and experts who might be able to help. She has found and organized her folks' insurance, business, and financial interests, as well as their personal papers and effects.

It is now time for her to shift the focus from one of

hunting and gathering to that of control and a formal process.

It's now time to go to court.

# Step 3. Petitioning the Court for Probate of the Estate

The first step Carolyn Goodwin has to take is to prepare and file the petition for probate in the court of competent jurisdiction. This petition process includes:

1. Submitting the original last will and testaments and the codicils (will changes) and certified copy of her parents' death certificates to the court clerk or probate registrar.
2. Obtaining an initial hearing date for the petition. This might have to be scheduled weeks or even months in the future.
3. Having herself appointed as administrator by filing an application for appointment with this court.

## PROVING THE WILL

Several years ago, a very, very, *very* rich man died. His named was Howard Hughes. After his passing, several "wills" surfaced, all alleging to be the true last will and testament of Mr. Hughes. One of these "wills" was the now-famous "Mormon Will," which became the subject of a Hollywood movie. Of all these "wills," which was his *true* last will and testament?

How does one verify that this will is the real last will and testament of the decedent and not some pretender? That is one of the jobs of the probate court. The process by which a will is deemed valid is called *proving*. This simply means that the will is accepted by the court as the last will and testament of the decedent and that it was executed (signed and witnessed) lawfully in the residence state of the decedent.

Some states allow for a last will and testament to be *self-proving*. This is when no further verification is required. Each state's requirements are outlined in Appendix I under will-proving requirements. To be absolutely sure about the state laws in your situation, contact the probate registrar or clerk of the probate court of competent jurisdiction.

## NOTIFICATION OF DEATH

The next task facing Carolyn is to notify all "interested parties" of the death of her parents. These can be defined as heirs, beneficiaries, creditors, trustees under a deed of trust, business associates, and anyone else that could possibly have an interest in her folks' affairs.

Depending on state law, notification can take one of two forms:

1. Deliver to the court a list (on an approved court form) of all interested parties. State laws direct who must receive notification and the requirements for delivery or mailing of that notice, which includes: delivery in person, certified mail, first-class mail, or registered mail.

In some states, court personnel are required to handle

this notification and will probably be done for a fee. In other states, the administrator, personal representative, executrix, or executor is responsible.

2. In addition to individual notification, most states require that the general public be notified as well. This usually takes the form of a notice placed in a newspaper with general circulation in the city or county where the decedent lived. This notice is different from the printed obituary.

All states set a time deadline for notification, whether by hand delivery, by mail, and/or by publication, and the number of times such notification must be published. The court will demand proof that such notification was accomplished within its guidelines and state laws. Some states will allow the combining of the creditor notice with individual and general public notice.

If there is a challenge to the will, it is most likely to come at this stage.

## ADMINISTRATION APPROVAL

After the last will and testament had been presented to the court and proper notifications made, Carolyn applied for appointment as "administrator." The administrator must be appointed and approved by the court, or by the heirs if the decedent did not name an individual or the individual named cannot or will not serve.

An executor or personal representative is usually named in a will. As both her parents died at the same time, and they had not made any provision for an alternate, that selection was made by the probate court.

Carolyn's petition to be the administrator could be

## NOTICE OF PETITION TO ADMINISTER ESTATE OF JOHN M. LUCERO, JR.

### Case No. BP038498

To all heirs, beneficiaries, creditors, contingent creditors, and persons who may be otherwise interested in the will or estate, or both, of JOHN M. LUCERO, JR.

A PETITION has been filed by Maida C. Foote in the Superior Court of California, County of LOS ANGELES.

THE PETITION requests that Maida C. Foote be appointed as personal representative to administer the estate of the decedent

THE PETITION requests authority to administer the estate under the Independent Administration of Estates Act. (This authority will allow the personal representative to take many actions without obtaining court approval. Before taking certain very important actions, however, the personal representative will be required to give notice to interested persons unless they have waived notice or consented to the proposed action.) The independent administration authority will be granted unless an interested person files an objection to the petition and shows good cause why the court should not grant the authority.

A HEARING on the petition will be held on February 7, 1996 at 9:15 AM in Dept. No. 5 located at 111 N. Hill St. Los Angeles, CA 90012.

IF YOU OBJECT to the granting of the petition, you should appear at the hearing and state your objections or file written objections with the court before the hearing. Your appearance may be in person or by your attorney.

IF YOU ARE A CREDITOR or a contingent creditor of the deceased, you must file your claim with the court and mail a copy to the personal representative appointed by the court within four months from the date of first issuance of letters as provided in section 9100 of the California Probate Code. The time for filing claims will not expire before four months from the hearing date noticed above.

YOU MAY EXAMINE the file kept by the court. If you are a person interested in the estate, you may file with the court a formal Request for Special Notice of the filing of an inventory and appraisal of estate assets or of any petition or account as provided in section 1250 of the California Probate Code. A Request for Special Notice form is available from the court clerk.

Attorney for petitioner:
**JAMES M. SAKRISON, Esq.**
*33 North Stone*
*#1100*
*Tucson, AZ 85701*
CN344151 LUCER Jan 17,18,24, 1996

challenged by an interested party, and once approved, that approval can be overturned.

No challenges were forthcoming and the judge issued documents called "letters of administration" that provided Carolyn with her authority. If she had been named under a will as executrix, she would have received "letters testamentary." The originals of these letters stay with the court and Carolyn uses certified copies in her day-to-day activities.

The administrator or executor or personal representative must post a bond. This protects the estate's assets from being "misplaced or misappropriated." Bonds may be obtained from a bonding company, insurance company, or a bank.

In most states, the administrator swears under oath under legal penalty to fairly and honestly settle the estate.


## ORDER FOR PROBATE

The probate court judge will sign an "order for probate." This is the beginning of the court-governed probate process; the state has now taken over control of the Goodwin estate. Carolyn is obliged to proceed exactly as directed by the court.

The clock is officially ticking.

Probate is a file-and-wait process. Certain things must be completed, and an inevitable amount of time must pass before the next step can be started.

# Step 4. Assemble and Inventory All Estate Assets

Carolyn Goodwin's first task was to itemize *all* of the assets in her parents' estate. Here is where her preliminary investigation and organizational ability will start to pay off. This must be done within a prescribed period of time. The window for this is set by state law and usually varies from four to ten months.

Some states require that all assets, whether under the jurisdiction of the court or not, be included in this inventory. One of the reasons for this is that in some states, the legal and other fees to be paid by the estate are based on the *gross* valuation of the estate and not just the probate valuation.

If Carolyn has not already opened up a bank account for the specific purpose of paying probate-related fees, now is the time to do so. She will pay *all costs* from this account and deposit *all income* into it.

It is ABSOLUTELY CRITICAL that ACCURATE records be kept by the administrator. Never commingle, mix together, a personal account with that of the estate. The court will require the administrator to account for every penny. If there is even a hint that improper accounting techniques are being used, Carolyn could be terminated as administrator and, where applicable, may be subject to further legal action—not only by the beneficiaries and creditors, but by the court as well.

Under court supervision, Carolyn will proceed to:

62

*Collect life insurance policies and cash. Secure tax waivers.*

1. Collect all life insurance and accidental death policies. She will make claims on her parents' deaths at this time. Each company will have its own evidence requirements, but each one will want to have original certified copies of her folks' death certificates.

A word about death certificates. Most if not all banks, financial institutions, county recorders, and insurance companies will require an original certified copy before they will release funds or property. Be sure to order as many as you think you will need, plus several more. If you run out, it could bring the probate process to a stop because it might take days or weeks to obtain more from the county clerk.

2. Pay ongoing insurance requirements, like the homeowner's and automobile policies, from the estate account.

3. Collect and account for all cash on the estate. This will be deposited into the estate account. Silver and gold coins are not considered cash, but rather investments and/or collections.

4. Speak to the family accountant about obtaining waivers on taxes such as business, inventory, quarterly withholding, income, or self-employment.

*Inventory and appraise personal property.*

In this step, Carolyn will be dealing directly with a court-appointed appraiser or "referee." It is this person's job to make sure that all the decedent's personal property is inventoried and valued. Depending on the nature of the assets, this step can get very expensive. If there are antiques, works of art, rare coin collections, artifacts, fine designer jewelry, collector cars, or other items of value exceeding the average, additional *independent* expert opinions of value will be required.

If the decedent owned only a partial interest in the asset, only his or her share will be included in the inventory.

Example: "A one-half (½) interest in the 1996 Freeway Eclipse 28′ Motor Home, Florida license 375TGH."

The court will supply the necessary form to use. It will probably be called a "schedule of assets" or "inventory and appraisal schedule." It will be filed with the court when complete.

*Claim for money due. Gain evidence and witnesses on contested claims.*

Before he was killed, Mr. Goodwin had made a $3,000 loan to one of his longtime employees. This loan was secured by the automobile title on the employee's car and a personal note. Carolyn had found these items and filed them in the estate settlement organizer she had prepared earlier. She was authorized by the probate court to continue receiving the monthly scheduled payments. These she deposited into the estate account and gave the debtor a receipt for the payment.

Debt can go in the other direction as well. If Mr. Goodwin had received a loan instead of giving one, that loan will need to be repaid *through the court*. What if the creditor computes one amount as being due, and the administrator comes up with a different amount? If agreement cannot be worked out, then you have a "contested claim" against the estate. The court will decide who is right.

Creditors have only a limited amount of time to file a claim against the estate. Once that time has passed, any creditor not having filed a claim is precluded from ever filing a claim. Since most debt is "secured," it is very rare for a large creditor of an estate—i.e., mortgage holder—not to file a claim within the allotted time frame.

*Arrange for supervision and management of ongoing business.*

This step is one of the most complicated and frustrating to accomplish. As stated before, running a business under court order and supervision is not conducive to smooth operations.

Carolyn Goodwin had never worked in her parents' business, but was now asked to run it! She was smart enough to know that she knew nothing about the dry cleaning business. Fortunately for Carolyn, the business was already managed by a longtime trusted employee. If no such person were available, she could have petitioned the court to allow her to hire a manager to run the business on behalf of the estate.

She collected the receipts on a daily basis and deposited them in the business account. She provided the bank with copies of her "letters of administration," allowing her to deposit and withdraw cash as the business required.

Many times, a business will have to be sold. There is a special type of professional you can use called business brokers. They will know how to inventory the business stock, value the fixtures, and even put a value on the "goodwill" generated by the business. You can find a business broker in the Yellow Pages, or ask the probate registrar for the name of a court-approved broker.

Sometimes a business will just close its doors. In Pennsylvania, a father died and willed his local small-town hardware store and all of the stock to his only child. She didn't know much about running a hardware store, so she just locked it up until she could better handle the challenge. In 1991, the daughter reopened the store, *fifty years after she had locked it!* What she had was not so much a hardware store as a time capsule from 1941. Many items were sold as "new in the box" antiques, and she made a small fortune.

*Gain custody of securities. Collect interest, dividends, and payments.*

This step of the assemble and inventory process will probably take longer to complete than the others. Whereas filing claims and collecting on life insurance policies, inventorying and appraising personal property, accounting for money due and owed by the estate, and arranging for the continued operation of a business might be accomplished in weeks or several months, it could take up to a year to gain enough information to fulfill the requirements of complete and total accounting. The main reason for this is a lack of estate organization on the part of the decedent. Some investments only pay a dividend or other payment annually—once a year, not quarterly. If the decedent kept incomplete records, you might not know of the existence of this asset for perhaps one full year. This is a very frustrating exercise to go through because there is no way you can expedite the process.

If the decedent worked with a stockbroker, financial planner, accountant, or other professional, you might not have to wait at all to gather all the information. All of the investments and securities might be in a single account managed by the financial professional. If this is the case, you will simply obtain the needed information from that person or institution.

You can also review the federal and state tax returns for the year prior to the decedent's passing. This can shed a lot of light on his or her asset holdings.

Even though you can discover a lot of information and knowledge about the decedent's stocks, bonds, and security investments, you will never really know if what you are seeing is everything he or she owned at the time of passing.

If the estate is low on working capital, you may ask the probate court for permission to sell off some of these assets in order to pay ongoing estate expenses. If a capital asset is sold at the market value of that asset as of the date or six months after the date of death, there will be no capital gain on the asset and no federal capital gain tax due. This is because the decedent received a tax break when he or she passed away called stepped-up basis. If the asset was owned jointly, then the decedent's share will receive a proportional step up in basis. Please review the joint ownership section earlier in this book.

If the decedent did not use the services of a stockbroker and had possession of actual stock certificates, you will have to contact the "transfer agent" hired by the certificate-issuing company to handle stock transactions on the company's behalf. Contact the issuing company or a broker to find out the name of the transfer agent. (It will usually be a bank or other financial institution.) In order to sell this stock, you will need to provide the transfer agent with the original certificate issued by the company, a certified copy of the decedent's death certificate, copy of the court order to sell, and a copy of your "letters of administration." You will also need to fill out the "power" declaration usually found on the back of the certificate. If it's not there, the transfer agent will provide one for you.

As sale proceeds of an asset, or interest income, dividends, and other payments, flow into the estate, deposit them into the estate account.

*Review condition, leases, taxes, and mortgage on real estate. Manage same.*

Though real estate is probably the largest part of the decedent's estate, it is one of the easiest asset types to manage. This is because it is the most "traceable" asset. All you will need to do is contact the county recorder to find out what real property the decedent owned outright. If real estate was owned through shares in a limited partnership, it could take a little more investigating.

Another reason real estate is fairly easy to deal with is that there are numerous professionals ready to assist you and provide the information you will need to satisfy the court.

Real estate brokers can provide you with information as to the market value of the property as of the date of death. They should provide this information at no charge to the estate, and will prepare what is called a comparative market analysis, or CMA. Many times, the court and the tax collector will accept a CMA for the establishment of a property's value. Please deal with licensed *brokers*, and not *agents*. There is a big difference in the two. Brokers have a higher degree of training and tend to be more dedicated to the real estate business.

If the court or the tax man will not accept a CMA, you will have to provide them with a formal appraisal of the property. If the property in question is a single-family home, the cost will be up to $300 or $400. If the property is income-producing, commercial, industrial, or vacant land, the appraisal costs are likely to be higher. Many times, the court will provide you with a list of approved appraisers from which you must choose one.

Another place to gather information is from a title insurance or guarantee company. These companies can provide you with information as to who owned what, when, and where. They can provide profiles of the decedent's real property and help establish ownership and answer other questions as well. For example, they know if a lien or other legal action has been filed against the property and if the taxes have been paid.

Speaking of property taxes, you might need to speak with the county tax assessor. Each time you call, speak with the same clerk or deputy. It will help things go a lot smoother.

If the property is leased or rented, you can contact a property management firm. They can be expensive, but with everything else you have to deal with, it may be worth it to hire one. They are usually paid out of the gross rent receipts due the estate. Check with the court before you commit to, and sign a contract with, any property management firm.

If the property is mortgaged or secured by a deed of trust, the holder of those instruments will need to be told of the owner's passing. In most cases, the mortgage, note, or trust deed will not be "accelerated," "called," or suddenly become all due and payable. However, this does not mean that you can stop making the payments. Payments will still be required in the same amount and on the same terms as when the decedent was living. You may have to sell other assets in the estate to make the monthly payments. Remember, probate can take one to two years or more to complete.

If the estate is cash poor, the real estate may have to be sold. Selling real estate held in probate is far more cumbersome then selling it outside this system. The court can put all manner of rules, regulations, limits, conditions, and guidelines on the sale of property that may not always benefit or expedite the sales process. In fact, some states have laws that prevent a family home from being sold if there is a surviving spouse or minor children. This can put tremendous financial strain on a family already reeling from the death of a loved one.

# Step 5. Obtain Appraisal of All Assets

Carolyn has now successfully assembled and inventoried all her parents' assets and personal property. She also now knows all of her parents' debts and money owed them.

But what is all this stuff worth? The court, beneficiaries, Uncle Sam, and the state tax man all want to know. There can be a lot of "inquiring minds" who also want to know. Remember that probate is a matter of public record, and the inventory and asset valuation will be open to anyone who wants to see them. There is no requirement for a reason or need to know. The Goodwin estate is an open book.

Appraising all the remainder of the assets is a distinct and separate step in the probate process. Even so, there should be a seamless progression from assembly and inventory to appraisal.

The probate court will provide you with a list of approved appraisers and/or referees. They work on behalf of the court, not the estate, and provide the court with an "independent" estimation of the value of the estate. The court may not accept a CMA on real property as discussed earlier. If you disagree with the court-appointed appraiser's or referee's figures and want to challenge their findings, the court will, in most cases, allow the personal representative, executor, executrix, or administrator to obtain a second appraisal. There could even be a situation in which the heirs might dispute the findings and direct the administrator to seek another opinion of value.

An appraisal is really nothing more than an opinion based on information about the asset. It is not uncommon for two appraisers to arrive at two different figures when appraising the same asset.

There is an added twist to the appraisal process that can slow down the entire probate proceeding ... yet save the estate many thousands of dollars in taxes! The IRS will allow one of two different dates to be used when arriving at the estimated value. The first date is the date the decedent died. The second is six months from that death date. When you are considering *income taxes* on the sale of capital assets, you will want the appraised value of the asset to be more or the same as the sales price. When you are considering the payment of *federal inheritance taxes*, you will want as low an assigned value as possible. Remember, the estate will receive a stepped-up basis on all capital assets and an estate under $600,000* pays no federal inheritance tax.

* The current personal estate exemption amount.

# Step 6: Administer the Estate

In this step, Carolyn will, through court supervision, manage the affairs of her parents' estate. This can include the day-to-day oversight of operating the family business and initiating the sale of assets to pay debts of the estate.

Do not confuse this single step of "administration" as it defines the day-to-day management of the estate with the global or big picture of "administration" as it defines what type of probate, supervised, unsupervised, small estate, or ancillary, the estate will be managed under.

Estate administration will follow one of three courses, with the potential for course crossover. These courses are administration by: the decedent's last will and testament, the needs of the estate, state law, or a combination of the three.

If the administration is by the will of the decedent, then the directions of the decedent will be followed. For instance, the decedent, through his will, might direct his personal representative or executor to turn over his home to his daughter. If everything goes according to plan, this transfer will ultimately take place.

If the administration is centered on the needs of the estate, there could be quite a different outcome. Instead of the home's being transferred to his daughter as directed in his will, it might have to be sold to pay debts of the estate. The needs, payment of the decedent's debts, take precedent over the directions of the decedent. The daughter would ultimately receive the net proceeds from that sale.

If state law is used as the basis for administration, the decedent's will could be completely disregarded and thrown out by the judge. If this were to happen, the daughter may be disinherited and her share of the estate given to someone else.

It is in this step that assets will be sold as directed by the court or by the needs of the estate. Carolyn will have to review the marketability for the potential sale for all estate assets, including the personal property, business interests, real estate, and securities.

She will complete or adjust for open contracts that her parents had, both personal and business. She will not pay any balances due on contracts until the next phase of probate.

Even though estate administration looks as if it is a single, one-time step, in reality the estate will have to be managed and administered for as long as it takes to:

1. Safeguard the state assets.
2. Petition the court for probate and make notifications.
3. Assemble and inventory all the estate's assets.
4. Obtain all appraisals.
5. Prepare all tax returns.
6. Settle all approved claims against the estate.
7. Distribute the estate.
8. Make the final accounting to the court.

As you can see, estate administration is the heart of the probate process, as it extends with varying degrees through all its phases.

# Step 7. Prepare All Tax Returns

At this point, assets of the estate will start to be used to pay taxes. Uncle Sam is *always* first in line for his "fair share" of the estate, whether it be inheritance tax, income tax, or the clearing of tax liens. Next in line are the state and local tax collectors. Depending on which state(s) the decedent owned property in, there may be additional estate or death taxes levied by that state. In states classified as "federal credit," "federal exempt," or "pick up," there are no additional estate taxes over and above those paid to the federal government upon the passing of an individual.

There are several forms of income taxes that may have to be paid. Both federal and state income taxes for the year prior to the decedent's passing, if not already filed, and for that portion of the current year in which the individual was still alive. Tax waivers will show the court that taxes have been paid.

The administrator may also have to pay the decedent's property taxes, both real and personal, plus business and inventory taxes. Permits may have to be renewed.

Please read the "Dealing with the Tax Man" section for complete details about federal and state taxes.

At this point, assets already cleared through probate such as securities and property owned by the decedent in other states can start to be distributed to the beneficiaries if taxes and debts have been satisfied.

# Step 8. Settle All Approved Claims

When Mr. and Mrs. Goodwin were killed in the accident, they owed money in various ways. These included the month-to-month bills such as utility, telephone, credit cards, and mortgage. There were also medical and funeral expenses. In addition, the dry cleaning business had creditors.

In her case, Carolyn had notified all known creditors and published general notices in the local paper per the instructions and guidelines of the probate court.

The administrator will collect the bills and submit to the court evidence of the creditors' outstanding debts. These are considered claims against assets in the estate. Evidence can take the form of a monthly billing, as in a utility bill, a note, as in a loan, or in a one-time billing, as in medical and funeral expenses.

In every state, creditors have only a certain period of time in which to attach the estate for repayment. Once that time frame has passed, the opportunity for repayment expires. At the end of this period, Carolyn collected all claims that had been presented to the probate court. A claim submitted after this deadline need not be paid, and any payment is made upon the goodwill of the administrator and the beneficiaries of the estate.

The next job is to determine the accuracy and validity of each claim. Monthly utility bills are simple enough to validate. However, you may dispute part or all of a creditor's claim. In this case, you will need to send that particular creditor a notice that the claim is in dispute and will be disallowed as presented. This notice must conform to court rules and be sent within a specific time frame. The creditor then has the opportunity to either accept your disallowance, accept partial payment as payment in full, or petition the court to allow the claim as first presented.

Most states allow small claims, like utility bills, to be paid outright. Be sure to account for these payments. For other types of claims (usually a large amount), the court will require that the waiting period pass and its permission given before that claim is paid.

There is a class of claim, called preferred or superior, that gets paid first before other claims and assets distributed. The claim that takes precedent over *all* other claims is for the attorney representing the estate. This will also apply to the personal representative or administrator and the funeral expenses.

## THEY SAID, "SELL IT . . . NOW!"

If there isn't enough cash in the estate, the probate court can go so far as to force the sale of assets in the estate in order to pay off a debt. For example, if that asset is real estate, there could be a forced sale in a down market. Consequently, that asset would not provide a maximum return and the dollar value of the estate would be substantially decreased. The same would hold true for stocks, bonds, business interests, art, collectibles, and anything else owned at the time of the decedent's passing. If the estate is debt free, the probate process itself becomes a debt against the estate and the estate assets can be forced to be sold to pay the court and lawyer's fees—*to pay the very people who are forcing the sale of the estate in the first place!*

# Step 9. Distribute Remainder of Estate

## SPECIAL BEQUESTS

Carolyn's mother had requested that upon her death, a portion of her estate be given to a humane organization. This is called a special bequest. A special bequest is a gift. It is generally an item of monetary value or specific dollar amount that may be distributed upon the passing of either husband or wife. Such bequests may come from separate property or from a joint estate. Special bequests, sometimes called specific bequests, are distributed prior to the division of the estate into shares for the beneficiaries' distribution.

I am reminded of the story about an older gentleman who had two lady friends, Anne and Suzy. These two ladies didn't like each other, but they both liked the old gentleman too much to risk having him choose between them.

In his last will and testament, he named Anne to be his personal representative, who would see to it that his estate was settled as he wanted.

After the old gentleman passed away, Anne read his will. It stated that he wanted to give a special bequest to Suzy in the following manner: "Please sell my Cadillac and give the full proceeds from that sale to Suzy." Taking her task very seriously, Anne phoned the local radio station and placed the following free ad on that station's "Bargain Box" show: "For Sale, 1995 Cadillac, low miles, $50." Well, Anne's phone started to ring immediately and the car was sold twelve minutes later to a handsome widower who lived just two blocks away.

The next day, she was driven over to Suzy's apartment by her handsome new boyfriend in his 1995 Cadillac and gave Suzy a check for the full $50, just as her old boyfriend requested.

## DISTRIBUTION OF ESTATE TO HEIRS OF GREG AND MARY GOODWIN

Carolyn Goodwin and her family have gone through a great deal of effort to get to this point. All the statutory notifications are completed, taxes paid, valid creditor claims paid, special bequests made, and the final accounting has been filed with the court.

If there were no last-minute objections, the next step would be to petition the court for permission to distribute the balance of the estate to the beneficiaries. This distribution will take one of six forms, or a combination of them.

1. A "life estate" is one that may be bequeathed to an individual or organization. A life estate is also called an "estate for years." It gives the recipient the use of an item, often real estate, for a certain number of years or for his or her lifetime. When that time limit is fulfilled, the asset goes to the "remainderman," that person who inherits the asset at the termination of the life estate holder's interest.

2. A particular asset, like a numbered bank account

or stock fund, is given to the beneficiary. There is danger in giving particular assets, because if that asset is sold to pay expenses or no longer exists as an estate asset, the named beneficiary of that asset will be inadvertently disinherited.

3. A specific dollar amount is to be paid to a named individual. What if the estate has been depleted to such an extent that the amount stated no longer exists or, worse yet, makes up a significant percentage of the remainder of the estate? It could happen, and does, that only one beneficiary will inadvertently get the lion's share.

4. If the decedent left no last will and testament, the laws of intestate succession in the decedent's residence state will dictate who the heirs are and what they will receive.

5. "In kind" distribution, allowed in most states, is when an heir receives physical assets of an estate valued in the same amount as if the asset were sold and the cash given to that person. Occasionally, in kind distribution will be disallowed: when the heirs request that the asset remains in the estate; when the heirs request a cash distribution, or the market value of the asset is less than the cash distribution would be.

6. The final, and best, way to allocate the remainder of the estate is through the use of shares or percentages. You can be sure that the final assets will be split using this method.

Under the Uniform Probate Code, if a beneficiary of the estate is a minor or incompetent, his or her share will, if over $5,000, be given to that person's parents or guardian to be held in trust for the benefit of that child or incompetent. This usually takes the form of a savings account or other low-risk investment.

Always get a receipt from the recipient that he or she in fact received their full inheritance. Any assets that are improperly distributed may be recalled by court action.

It is usually a straightforward process to distribute large asset items to the beneficiaries. It is quite a different story for personal items owned by the decedent. It is common for serious arguments to break out between brothers and sisters over small items of jewelry or an heirloom after Mom or Dad has passed away.

# Step 10. Closing the Probate and Obtaining Final Discharge

This is the moment that each and every personal representative, administrator, executor, or executrix longs for. There is light at the end of the tunnel.

Carolyn Goodwin is no exception to this rule. She is coming to the end of over two years of battling bureaucracy, discovery, inventory, accounting, claims, running a business, paying taxes, and sibling rivalry. All payments have been made and all assets distributed. It is now time to wrap it up.

Carolyn delivers to the court all the distribution records and receipts, hundreds of papers, forms, the final accounting, and a petition to be discharged as administrator of her parents' estate.

After a waiting period, the judge discharges Carolyn

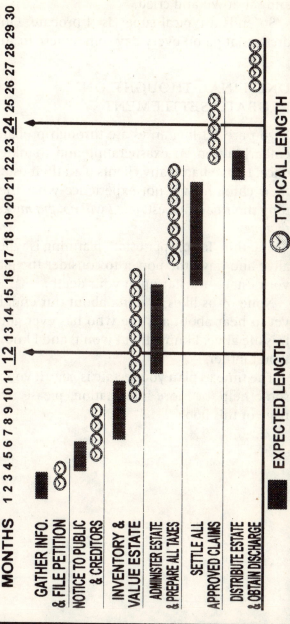

# THE PROBATE PROCESS

**MONTHS** 1 2 3 4 5 6 7 8 9 10 11 <u>12</u> 13 14 15 16 17 18 19 20 21 22 23 <u>24</u> 25 26 27 28 29 30

GATHER INFO. & FILE PETITION

NOTICE TO PUBLIC & CREDITORS

INVENTORY & VALUE ESTATE

ADMINISTER ESTATE & PREPARE ALL TAXES

SETTLE ALL APPROVED CLAIMS

DISTRIBUTE ESTATE & OBTAIN DISCHARGE

⊘ TYPICAL LENGTH

■ EXPECTED LENGTH

from her duties. She received her discharge in the mail and sat down and cried.

So ends a typical supervised probate. One of hundreds that go on every day somewhere in America.

## ONE FINAL THOUGHT ON PROBATE SETTLEMENT

If you are settling an estate through probate, you are embarking on an exasperating and thankless experience. I have had many clients plan their estates so that their children will not experience what they did settling their parents' estate. *"I will not put my kids through that mess."*

The time for proper estate planning is when you are alive and have the power to consider the planning for your estate transfer upon your death.

None of us likes to think about our end, but I have yet to hear about anyone who has ever gotten out of this life alive. I know that I won't, and I know that you won't either.

The time to plan your estate is *now*. If you would like some help, or more information, please read the last page of this book.

# 5. Estate Settlement by Trust (Living Trust)

The fifth and final way an estate can be settled and the assets transferred to the decedent's heirs is through the use of a trust. This is how John Hook will settle his father's estate. Trusts have been used for many years by the more affluent in our country. It is only within the past ten years that their use has "trickled down" to the rest of us.

By far, the most widely employed trust is that of the living trust, also called an inter vivos trust, family trust, grantor trust, or estate planning trust. The living trust has become quite popular and the settlement vehicle of choice by millions of individuals and families throughout America.

## What Is a Living Trust?

A living trust is a document created during one's lifetime whereby that person sets up the mechanism to retain full control of their assets and, upon their passing, transfer those assets to the chosen heirs quickly and privately without court permission. It is usually revocable, meaning that during his or her lifetime that person may alter any of its terms and even cancel the trust completely. Upon their passing, either part or all of the trust becomes irrevocable.

An irrevocable living trust is just that, irrevocable. The terms and conditions of this type of trust cannot be modified or revoked except, under certain conditions, by court order.

The great benefits of a trust are that they avoid costly probate court costs and lawyers' fees and save on taxes. In addition, the family maintains control over the management and distribution of an estate to its heirs.

## Trust Estate Settlement

Settling an estate by trust is a much "friendlier" process to go through than probate. There are two huge differences between a last will and testament and a living trust:

1. *A will must be probated, a living trust avoids probate.* With a living trust, control remains with the family, and estate asset allocation and distribution are not lost to the court bureaucracy and lawyers. A living trust settlement is a family matter, the public is not able to snoop into the decedent's private affairs. Since the living trust avoids probate, it also avoids all the court and legal fees imposed by that process. Everything you need to settle the decedent's estate will be right there at your fingertips—all information and the power to act. With a properly drawn living trust, and the decedent's estate organized, you should be able to settle the estate in one hour.

84

*2. Income, federal inheritance, and state estate tax savings.*

With a properly drawn living trust, and all of the decedent's major assets "owned" by his or her trust, there is potential for some rather significant tax savings.

These are outlined in the "Dealing with the Tax Man" section of this book.

# The First Step

After his father's funeral, John went to the local bank to retrieve the contents of his dad's safe deposit box. Along with a few gold coins, stock certificates, and the deed to the house, John found his father's living trust document.

As with any estate settlement process, John's first task was to get organized. As stated earlier, organization is the key to smooth estate settlement. The organizing of an estate by trust is similar to that of an estate by will. Many of the discovery and organizational steps are the same.

Please review the "Step 1. Locate and Read the Will" section presented earlier in this book. It will provide you with the general guidelines needed to start a trust

---

* In 1994, Iowa enacted a law that treats living trusts as "testamentary" trusts. This means that the trust will take effect only upon the death of the grantor, and regards trust assets as if they are a part of the gross probate estate for the purposes of calculating court, lawyer, and other fees.

estate settlement. Change the word "will" to "trust" and ignore *all* references to probate.

One big difference in reading a trust is that a properly drawn living trust should be between twenty and fifty pages in length, as opposed to a will, which may be only one or two pages. So look for a larger document, or even a set of papers.

# Successor Trustee (Who Is in Control?)

When John reads the trust document, he will look for and pay particular attention to the "successor trustee" section or clause. In it, he will find the person or persons designated to take over control of the estate after the passing of the decedent.

This section should read something like this:

> In the event of the death of the original Trustee, William Hook, or if for any reason such person ceases to serve as Trustee hereunder, the Trustor, William Hook, nominates and appoints John Hook to serve as Successor Trustee hereunder without the approval of any court.

This means that John has complete control over his father's estate and the settling of his affairs. He needs no court approvals, policies, or intervention of any kind.

He is put in charge and empowered by the trust language. If something happens to John and he cannot, or will not, serve, his dad named an alternate successor trustee.

# Who Gets What, When, How, and Other Distribution Issues

The next sections John will read are the beneficiary, allocation, and distribution sections. These sections act much like a last will and testament in that they state:

1. Who the beneficiaries (heirs) of the decedent's trust estate are.
2. What they are to receive, either by share, value, or asset.
3. When they are to receive their inheritance to do with as they please.

Other subsections or clauses will enlighten John and give him insight on how to handle any special circumstances, distributions, and asset management situations that may arise over the years as they relate to any heirs' beneficial interest in the trust estate.

The Trustees shall allocate, hold, administer and distribute the Trust assets as hereinafter delineated.

# What Happened When Mr. Hook Died?

Upon the passing of the decedent, William Hook, all or a portion of the trust estate assets can be distributed to that decedent's beneficiaries.

If married, all assets would usually remain held in the trust for the benefit of the surviving spouse.

> Upon the death of the Settlor, William Hook, the Trustee shall make any separate distributions that have been specified by the deceased Settlor. The Trustee shall also take into consideration the appropriate provisions of this section.

# Personal Property Distribution (Great-Grandma's Wedding Ring)

The elder Mr. Hook used the following technique to distribute small personal items, like his wedding ring or a family heirloom. This distribution technique is not to be used for major trust assets.

The Settlor requests the Trustee to abide by any *memorandum* by the Settlor directing the disposition of personal and household effects of every kind including but not limited to furniture, appliances, furnishings, pictures, china, silverware, glass, books, jewelry, wearing apparel, and all policies of fire, burglary, property damage, and other insurance on or in connection with the use of this property. Otherwise, the personal and household effects of the Settlor shall be distributed with the remaining assets of the trust estate.

# What If a Beneficiary Is a Minor?

Customarily, all assets of the trust estate remain in trust until the youngest heir attains the age of twenty-one. This is done to keep the entire trust estate intact for the beneficial needs of all minor beneficiaries until they reach majority. In the event of an unusual occurrence, such as an extended illness, the entire trust estate would be available to serve those specific needs of that minor child. When the youngest child attains age twenty-one, the trust estate will be available for allocation and distribution per the instructions set forth in the document.

When the youngest child of the Settlor, who is living, attains the age of 21, the Trustee shall divide the trust estate as then constituted into separate shares as hereinafter specified. This provision shall also apply to those shares allocated to the issue of a deceased primary beneficiary (as hereinafter designated).

# Keeping Well and Getting Educated

As successor trustee, John Hook is empowered to use trust estate assets to pay for continuation of any beneficiary's education.

At any time prior to the division of the Trust into shares as hereinbefore provided, or prior to distribution if divided, the Trustee may, at his sole and absolute discretion, provide such sums as shall be necessary or advisable, for the care and maintenance, medical needs, and education of any primary beneficiary. This provision shall also apply to the issue of a deceased primary beneficiary.

# Special Distribution (Seed Money)

With this clause, the elder Mr. Hook granted the successor trustee (at his/her discretion) the power to provide funds to pay for special objectives of any beneficiary of this trust, such as brothers and sisters. However, these payments will not diminish the allocated shares of any other beneficiary.

The Trustee is further authorized, in his sole and absolute discretion, to provide such sums as shall be necessary or advisable, for the furtherance of worthwhile personal, professional or business goals, and if deemed appropriate by the Trustee, to provide such reasonable sums for a partial or complete down-payment on a home of any primary beneficiary, provided, however, that no such aid or support shall in any way diminish the benefits available to any other beneficiary. Such provision shall also apply to the issue of a deceased primary beneficiary of a Settlor.

# Is It a Gift or a Loan?

John's father had made gifts and loans from the trust estate to his other children. He recorded which was a gift made outright and which was a loan to be repaid by the recipient. Any nonpayment can be deducted from a beneficiary's allocated share.

> The Trustee(s) shall reduce a beneficiary's share by any gifts or outstanding loans as shown in Schedule A.

# Handicapped Beneficiary (State Aid Can Be Costly)

Mr. Hook created his living trust for these main reasons:

1. Avoid government intrusion via the probate court.
2. Provide privacy to his family and in his affairs.
3. Obtain income tax benefits through the trust.
4. Where applicable, minimize inheritance and estate tax liability.

In short, he wanted to keep it all (or as much as he possibly could) in the family. This next clause helps to further accomplish this estate planning goal.

What if one of his beneficiaries were to become handicapped and eligible for government benefits? He would not want to jeopardize that person's (government) benefits. Nor would he want to give Uncle Sam, or the state, the right to reach in and confiscate that beneficiary's share for repayment of those benefits.

To prevent either of these occurrences from happening, Mr. Hook can remove that beneficiary from his trust and "disinherit" him or her. At the same time, the trustee is authorized, at their sole discretion, to provide whatever indirect funds are needed to provide personal care and maintenance for this handicapped individual.

In addition, he provided that should such handicapped individual recover, that person is automatically reinstated as a beneficiary.

Any beneficiary who is determined by a court of competent jurisdiction to be incompetent shall not have any discretionary rights of a beneficiary with respect to this Trust, or their share or portion thereof. The Trustee shall hold and maintain such incompetent beneficiary's share of the trust estate and shall, in the Trustee's sole discretion, distribute for and provide for such beneficiary as provided for in this Trust for benefits to minors, and under "Support and Education of the Beneficiaries."

Notwithstanding the foregoing, any beneficiary who is diagnosed for the purposes of governmental benefits (as hereinafter delineated) as being not competent or as being disabled, and who shall be entitled to governmental support and benefits by any reason of such incompetency or disability, shall cease to be a beneficiary of this Trust. Likewise, they shall cease to be a beneficiary if any share or portion of the principal or income of the Trust shall become subject to the claims of any governmental agency for costs or benefits, fees or charges.

The portion of the trust estate which, absent the provisions of this section "Handicapped Beneficiaries," would have been the share of such incompetent or handicapped person shall be retained in Trust for as long as that individual lives. The Trustee, at the sole discretion of the Trustee, may utilize such funds for the individual as specified under "Support and Education of the Beneficiaries." Upon the death of this individual the residual of this share shall be distributed as otherwise specified in the Trust.

If such individual recovers from incompetency or disability, and is no longer eligible for aid from any governmental agency, including costs or benefits, fees or charges, such individual shall be reinstated as a beneficiary after sixty (60) days from such recovery, and the allocation and distribution provisions as stated herein shall apply to that portion of the trust estate which is held by the Trustee subject to the foregoing provisions of this section.

If said handicapped beneficiary is no longer living and shall leave issue then living, the deceased handicapped beneficiary's share shall pass to said issue then living, equally. If there is no issue, such share shall be allocated proportionately among the remaining named beneficiaries. Each share shall be distributed or retained in Trust as hereinafter provided.

# Primary Beneficiaries
## (Who Gets an Inheritance)

In this clause, John is able to identify who his father's heirs, or "primary beneficiaries," are.

> Unless otherwise herein provided, upon or after the death of the Settlor, William Hook, the primary beneficiaries of this Trust are John Hook, James Hook, Jacob Hook, and Sara Jane Hook.

# Special Bequest
## (Who Gets a Special Gift)

As you will remember, a special bequest is a gift, and is generally an item of monetary value or specific dollar amount that may be distributed upon the passing of the decedent. Special, or specific, bequests are distributed prior to the division of the trust estate into shares for the primary beneficiaries.

The following special bequests shall be made by the Trustee and distributed outright upon the death of the Settlor: Two thousand ($2,000) each to Michigan State University and the University of Southern California for use as each university so decides.

# Allocation of Trust Assets (What the Primary Beneficiaries Are to Receive)

Allocation deals with the way in which Mr. Hook wishes to have his estate divided among the beneficiaries at his passing. In addition, he can provide that each primary beneficiary may be given an equal share or an unequal share of the trust estate assets.

Upon the death of the Settlor, William Hook, and after the debts and other obligations and provisions of the trust estate have been satisfied and any special distributions and retentions have been made, the Trustee shall allocate the balance of the trust estate as then constituted into three (3) equal and separate shares as to provide one (1) share for each of the primary beneficiaries of this trust agreement.

# Distribution of Trust Assets (When and How the Inheritance Is Distributed)

In this section, John will be instructed as to how his father wants the trust estate to be distributed to his children.

There are a number of ways these assets may be distributed, and the form this takes will determine how the decedent's beneficiaries will take possession. The most common means of distribution are:

1. Outright distribution upon the passing of the surviving spouse.
2. Distribution of income only, with assets retained in trust to be distributed at a later date.
3. Deferred distribution at predetermined ages.
4. Distribution on a partial basis over a period of time.

Mr. Hook chose an outright means of distribution.

Upon the death of the Settlor, William Hook, the Trustee shall distribute the trust estate allocated to the primary beneficiaries outright as soon as is practicable. Upon the death of a primary beneficiary, the Trustee shall distribute the undistributed balance of the Estate as specified in other applicable provisions herein included.

# Per Stirpes (Keeping It in the Bloodline)

What would happen in the event one of Mr. Hook's designated primary beneficiaries is not living at the time of his or her distribution? If that primary beneficiary has children (issue), that portion of the trust estate allocated to the primary beneficiary will be distributed in equal shares to all living children of that deceased primary beneficiary. So if John Hook had died before his father, John's children would receive his share. If John had no children, his brothers and sister would receive his share.

The legal term for such form of distribution is "per stirpes" (pronounced: *per stir-peas*) and it applies to the issue of any designated beneficiary.

Typical distribution to such living issue will be split into three parts. However, one can also distribute any share outright.

After division into shares pursuant to the paragraph "Allocation of Trust Assets" above, upon the death of a primary beneficiary of a Settlor prior to complete distribution of his or her share, the undistributed balance of such primary beneficiary's share shall be distributed per stirpes to his or her then living issue in the following manner: when such an heir (issue of a deceased primary beneficiary) attains the age of twenty-five (25) years, the Trustee shall distribute to such beneficiary one-third (⅓) of the principal of his or her share as then constituted; and when an heir (issue of a deceased primary beneficiary) attains the age of thirty (30) years, the Trustee shall distribute to such beneficiary one-half (½) of the principal of his or her share as then constituted; and when an heir (issue of a deceased primary beneficiary) attains the age of thirty-five (35) years, the Trustee shall distribute to such beneficiary the undistributed balance of his or her share. If an heir (issue of a deceased primary beneficiary) has already attained age twenty-five (25), age thirty (30), or age thirty-five (35) at the time this Trust is divided into shares, the Trustee shall, upon making the division, distribute to such beneficiary one-third (⅓), two-thirds (⅔) or all of his or her share, respectively. If a deceased primary beneficiary should leave no issue, then said deceased primary beneficiary's share shall be distributed per stirpes to the Settlor's then living issue.

# Intestate Succession

The laws of intestate succession apply only when all named beneficiaries and their issue are deceased at the time of the distribution of the decedent's estate. Upon such occurrence, the estate would be distributed to living family members such as the decedent's brothers, sisters, nieces, nephews, etc. (See chart on page 125, "Intestate Succession.") One can name other individuals instead of family members.

> If at the time of the Settlor's death, or at any later time prior to final distribution hereunder, all of the Settlor's beneficiaries are deceased and no other disposition of the property is directed by this Trust, then and in that event the then remaining property of this Trust shall be distributed to the Settlor's heirs by right of intestate succession.

# Charity

Mr. Hook could have elected to circumvent the above intestate succession clause by naming specific charities he selected to receive the balance of his trust estate instead of "upline" family members.

> If no such heirs are extant, then the Trustee is directed to distribute the property to qualified nonprofit charitable organizations identified in Schedule B. If no such charity is identified in Schedule B, the Trustee shall select appropriate nonprofit charitable organizations for distribution of the trust estate.

After reading these clauses in his father's trust, John now knows exactly how to use, allocate, and distribute *all* of the estate. Every contingency is covered. He does not have to speculate as to a course of action to follow, given any number of events taking place. He is not burdened with a "what if" situation.

He can turn his full attention to the discovery and management issues of settling his father's living trust estate.

# Trust Estate Management

Once the trust document is read, John will move immediately to organizing, safeguarding, assembling, and inventorying the assets of the estate. Please review the *"Step 2. Safeguarding Estate Assets"* and *"Step 4. Assemble and Inventory All Estate Assets"* sections earlier in this book. They will provide a guideline and insight into these processes. Change the word "will" to "trust" and you can ignore completely *all* references to probate.

Disregard *"Step 3. Petitioning the Court for Probate of the Estate"* as it does not apply to the settling of a trust estate, insofar as all major assets are "owned" by the trust, as are any assets outside the protection of the trust that are below the probate trigger figure for the state of residence of decedent as outlined in Appendix I.

John knows exactly what he has to do and how to do it. Since settling an estate through a living trust is an unsupervised process, John sets his own schedule, pace, and method for managing his father's estate, paying the bills and distributing the remainder of the estate to his brothers and sister. Please review "*Step 5. Obtain Appraisal of All Assets,*" "*Step 6: Administer the Estate,*" "*Step 7. Prepare All Tax Returns,*" "*Step 8. Settle All Approved Claims,*" and "*Step 9. Distribute Remainder of Estate*" for a general overview of the steps John Hook will take to settle this estate. Again, ignore all references to probate, waiting periods, forms to file with the court, court approvals, forced sale of assets, and any other items that refer to court control of the settlement process. They do not apply to a living trust estate settlement.

In fact, John does not have to go to court or file forms. He takes advantage of fluid markets and sells assets when they are high in value. He does not have to wait mandated lengths of time or get permission before he can act. He is in charge and can "strike while the iron is hot."

John need not even stay in Chicago to settle his father's estate. He can accomplish everything from the comfort of his own home in Portland, Oregon.

Before he leaves Chicago, he hires a real estate broker to market his dad's home. Three months later* the sale of the home is completed. John pays the estate's bills, creditor claims, and taxes. He then divides the net remainder of the estate equally among himself and his brothers and sister.

With that, the settlement of Mr. William Hook's estate is complete and John finishes the process with a feeling of accomplishment.

---

* Depending on market conditions, deferred distribution plans, and/or needs of the trust estate, this time could be shorter, longer, or significantly longer in your particular case.

# All the Power and Authority to Act

If William Hook had made a last will and testament instead of a living trust, the power to settle his estate would have gone to the lawyers and the probate court.

As Mr. Hook had the foresight to create a living trust, the power to act stays within the family. This authority is provided to the successor trustee through a series of "enabling" clauses contained in the trust document under the section heading of "Trustee Powers." The more defined the clauses, the better the ability to make things happen, with less chance of conflicting actions.

This section provides John with all the instructions and tools necessary to settle the estate. It is the blueprint for a speedy, smooth-running, and hassle-free settlement process that will take a fraction of the time and expense a typical probate takes.

The "trustee powers" section of the trust you are using may look different from the one presented here. They can take the form of a listing of general assets management functions such as taking care of real estate transactions, tangible personal property transactions, bond exchanges, share exchanges, commodity exchanges, financial institution transactions, business operating transactions, insurance transactions, claims and litigation, tax matters, benefits from military service and other estate transactions.

# Trustee Powers

As a successor trustee, John will need to make use of all the power granted to him in the trust document. Mr. Hook's intent was to make certain his son would not lose control of the estate's assets, but to enhance them. The clauses in this section are the cornerstone of the elder Mr. Hook's control over his estate while alive and his ability to transfer this power base to his son John. Thus, as shown below, John can actively manage the trust estate on behalf of the beneficiaries.

> **The Trustee shall have the following powers, duties, and discretions in addition to those otherwise granted herein or by law, and expected as elsewhere herein specifically restricted.**

# Trust Property

This clause gives the trustee power over trust-owned property and the authority to use that property.

> **The Trustee shall have no more extensive power over any property transferred to the Trust than the Settlor would have under the property laws of the situs state, had this Trust not been**

created, and this instrument shall be so interpreted to achieve this intention.

The Trustee shall hold, manage, invest, and reinvest the trust estate (if any requires such management and investment) and shall collect the income, if any, therefrom and shall dispose of the net income and principal during the life of the Settlor (William Hook) as follows:

The Trustee shall pay to, or apply for the benefit of the Settlor, all the net income of the estate.

The Trustee may pay to, or apply for the benefit of the Settlor, such sums from the principal of the trust estate as in its sole discretion shall be necessary or advisable from time to time for the medical care, welfare, and maintenance of the Settlor, taking into consideration to the extent the Trustee deems advisable any other income or resources of the Settlor known to the Trustee.

The Settlor may, at any time during the life of the Settlor, and from time to time, withdraw all or any part of the principal of the trust estate, free of Trust.

# General Property Powers

Why does John Hook not need to ask permission of anyone at anytime in the settling of this estate? It's because the following clauses provide an extensive range of power and latitude of judgment on the part of the trustee.

The Trustee shall have all such powers and is/ are authorized to do all such acts, take all such proceedings and exercise all such rights and privileges in the management of the trust estate as if the absolute owner thereof, including, without limiting the generality of the terms, the right to manage, control, sell, convey, exchange, partition, assign, divide, subdivide, improve, or repair; to grant options and to sell upon deferred payments; to lease for terms within or extending beyond the duration of the Trust concerned for any purpose, including the exploration for and removal of oil, gas, and other minerals; to enter into community oil leases, pooling and unitization agreement; to create restrictions, easements, and other servitudes; to compromise, arbitrate, or otherwise adjust claims in favor of or against the Trust; to institute, compromise, and defend actions and proceedings at the expense of the trust estate; and to carry such insurance as the Trustee may deem advisable.

# Power Regarding Securities, Options, and Investments

John, as successor trustee, will be dealing with brokerage houses in the sale of his father's securities, exercising options, and making investments on behalf of the trust and for the benefit of the beneficiaries. These brokerage houses will need the following powers, provided by the trust document, to be given to John so that he can make transactions in these areas.

The Trustee shall have, respecting securities, all the rights, powers, and privileges of an owner, including the right to vote stock, give proxies, pay assessments, and other sums deemed by the Trustee to be necessary for the protection of the trust estate; to participate in voting Trusts, pooling agreements, foreclosures, reorganizations, consolidations, mergers, and liquidations, and in connection therewith, to deposit securities with and transfer title to any protective or other committee under such terms as the Trustee may deem advisable; to exercise or sell stock subscription or conversion rights; to open an account with a brokerage firm of the choosing of the Trustee in the Trustee's name, in its own behalf for the purpose of purchasing and selling of all kinds of securities and authorizing such brokerage firm to act upon any orders, including margin orders, options, both covered and uncovered, instructions with respect to such accounts and/or the delivery of securities or money therefrom and received from said Trustee; and to retain as an investment any securities or other property received through the exercise of any of the foregoing powers. The Trustee is further authorized to sign, deliver, and/or receive any documents necessary to carry out the powers contained within this paragraph.

## OPTIONS

The Trustee is expressly authorized in the Trustee's sole discretion to exercise any option to purchase stock under any stock option purchaseplan in which a beneficiary is a participant or may hold such option rights to the extent that any such option rights may be exercised by the Trustee even though the stock involved is stock of a corporation which may be serving as corporate Trustee hereunder, regardless of the amount of such stock or the percentage of the trust estate which may be invested in such stock before or after any purchase under such option.

## INVESTMENTS
### General Powers

The Trustee has the power to invest and reinvest principal and income, to purchase or acquire therewith every kind of property, real, personal, or mixed, and every kind of investment, specifically including, but not by way of limitation, shares in one or more mutual funds, in any Common Trust Funds administered by the Trustee, corporate obligations of every kind, and stock, preferred or common, which persons of prudence and discretion and intelligence acquire for their own accounts.

The Trustee is/are further authorized to buy, sell, and trade in securities of any nature (including short sales) on margin, and for such purposes may maintain and operate margin accounts with brokers, and may pledge any securities held or purchased by them with such brokers as security for loans and advances made to the Trustee.

### Life Insurance and Annuities

The Trustee is authorized in the Trustee's discretion to maintain and/or purchase policies of life insurance and/or annuities on the life or for the benefit of any Trust beneficiaries and to hold and pay for the same as an investment and asset of the Trustee, at any time and upon successive occasions, the premiums to be charged against income or principal, as the Trustee shall determine.

The Trustee shall have the following powers, duties, and discretions with respect to policies of life insurance held as a part of the trust estate:

The Trustee may pay premiums, assessments, or other charges with respect so such policies together with all other charges upon such policies or otherwise required to preserve them as binding contracts, but shall be under no duty to do so.

In the event that the Trustee intends/intend not to pay any premium, assessment or other charge with respect to any policy held by it, or otherwise intends to cancel, convert, or substantially modify any such policy, it shall first give the insured, or the guardian of the person of an insured under disability, at least fifteen (15) days' advance written notice of its intention to take such action.

Any amounts received by the Trustee with respect to any policy as a dividend shall be treated as principal.

Upon the receipt of proof of death of any person whose life is insured for the benefit of any Trust hereunder, or upon maturity of any policy payable to the Trustee prior to the death of the insured, the Trustee shall collect all sums payable with respect thereto and shall thereafter hold such sums as principal of the respective trust estate, except that any interest paid by the insurer for a period subsequent to maturity shall be considered as income.

The Trustee may accept any payments due it under any settlement arrangement made before or after the death of the insured and may exercise any rights available to it under such arrangement.

The Trustee may compromise, arbitrate, or otherwise adjust claims upon any policies, and may, but shall not be required to, exercise any settlement options available under such policies. The receipt of the Trustee to the insurer shall be a full discharge and the insurer is not required to see to the application of the proceeds.

# Determination of Income and Principal

As successor trustee, John controls any and all income generated by trust assets and how those funds are to be spent.

The Trustee shall have the power and the authority to determine income and principal, and show receipts and disbursements, including the fees of the Trustee, shall be credited, charged, or apportioned as between income and principal; however, all such determination shall be made in accordance with the law of the state of the situs of the Trust and the decision and the accounts of the Trustee in accordance with said provisions shall be binding on all persons in interest.

Notwithstanding the foregoing, the Trustee shall: (1) allocate to principal all dividends or other payments made by any corporation or mutual investment company that are designated by the company as distribution of capital gains; (2) where a premium has been paid or a discount received in connection with the purchase of a bond, amortize such premium or discount by making an appropriate charge or credit to income as the case may be; and (3) charge income from time to time with a reasonable reserve for (a) depreciation of all income producing

III

depreciable real or personal property, and capital improvements and extraordinary repairs on income-producing property; (b) depletion of all depletable natural resources; and (c) all intangible property having a limited economic life. Such allocations and charges need not be made, however, if written consents are obtained from all income beneficiaries and remaindermen, vested or contingent, living and competent to act.

# Authority to Borrow and Encumber

John Hook even has the power to make a loan *to* or a loan *from* the trust, and use trust assets as collateral and security for said loans. This ability would be unheard-of if the estate were under the jurisdiction of the probate court.

The Trustee shall have the power to borrow money for any Trust purpose upon such terms and conditions as the Trustee may deem proper, and to obligate the trust estate for repayment and to encumber the trust estate or any of its property by mortgage, deed of Trust, pledge, or otherwise, using such procedure to consummate the transaction as the Trustee may deem advisable.

In addition to the power to encumber property for a loan being made to the Trust, the Trustee is/are specifically authorized and empowered to obligate, hypothecate, and encumber the trust estate by mortgage, deed of Trust, pledge or otherwise, or whatever form the Trustee deem appropriate, or to act as a third party guarantor to guarantee private borrowings of the Trustors or either of them during their joint lifetime. Upon the death of a Settlor, such guarantee may only be made from the Survivor's Trust A.

## LOANS
### To Trust
The Trustee shall have the power to, in the Trustee's discretion, advance funds to any Trust herein created for any Trust purpose, such advances with interest at current rates to be a first lien on and be paid out of the principal and as expense of the Trust; and to reimburse the Trustee from principal or accumulated income for any loss or expense incurred by reason of a Trustee's ownership or holding of any property in this Trust.

### To Beneficiaries
The Trustee may, at any time and upon successive occasions, loan such sums to the beneficiaries or any of them as the Trustee shall deem advisable and in the best interest of the

beneficiaries, such loan or loans, if made, to bear interest at the prevailing rate and to be unsecured or secured, as the Trustee may, in the Trustee's discretion, direct, provided, however, that the Trustee shall have wide discretion in making or denial of any such loan, and the Trustee's judgment in the matter shall be conclusive and binding on any beneficiary requesting any such loan.

# Distributions to or for Minor or Incompetent

If John were dealing with a situation in which a minor or incompetent is a beneficiary, he can still control how the distribution to that minor or incompetent is to be made. The court need not get involved.

If at any time any beneficiary entitled to receive income and/or principal hereunder shall be a minor or an incompetent or a person whom the Trustee deems to be unable, wisely or properly, to handle funds if paid to him or her directly, the Trustee may make any such payments, in the Trustee's discretion, in any one or more, or any combination, of the following ways:

Directly to such beneficiary, or

To the natural guardian or the legally appointed guardian, conservator, or other fiduciary of the person or estate of such beneficiary, or

To any person or organization furnishing support for such beneficiary, or

By the Trustee retaining the principal and making expenditures directly for the support of such beneficiary.

The Trustee shall not be required to see to the application of any funds so paid or applied, and the receipt of such payee if disbursed for such purpose in the best judgment of the Trustee shall be full acquittance to the Trustee. The decision of the Trustee as to direct payments or application of funds in the manner herein prescribed shall be conclusive and binding upon all parties in interest if made in good faith. The Trustee is/are requested to make all such disbursements in a way calculated to dispense with the necessity of guardianship proceedings.

The Trustee may, in its sole and absolute discretion, require such reports and take such steps as it may deem requisite to assure and enforce the due application of such money to the purposes aforesaid.

# Division of Trusts

The successor trustee has the power to determine asset values and division of those assets for the purposes of distribution.

In making the distributions to any Trust or share created under this Agreement, the judgment of the Trustee concerning the valuation of assets distributed shall be binding and conclusive upon all beneficiaries. The Trustee may distribute the shares to the various Trusts or to beneficiaries by making distribution in cash, or in kind, or partly in cash and partly in kind, or in undivided interest, in such manner as the Trustee, in its sole and absolute discretion, deems advisable. The Trustee may sell such property as it deems necessary to make any such division or distribution. The Trustee shall not be required to make physical division of the Trust property, except when necessary for the purposes of distribution, but may, in the Trustee's discretion, maintain and keep the assets of any separate Trusts in one or more consolidated Trust funds, and as to each consolidated Trust fund, the division into various shares comprising such Trust fund need to be made only upon the Trustee's books of account, in which each separate Trust shall be allotted its proportional share of the principal and income of the consolidated fund and shall be charged with its proportionate part of expenses thereof.

# Provisions for Taxes

In this clause, John is empowered to pay any and all type of taxes that may be due. When income taxes are due, he will simply file the appropriate schedule with the decedent's federal 706 and/or 1041 return, and, where applicable, state income tax forms. With an A single, A married, or A-B married living trust, those taxes will be due within nine months after the decedent's passing or that of the *first* spouse. Under an A-B-C trust, those taxes are due within nine months after the passing of the *surviving* spouse.

What if the trust estate has insufficient funds on hand to pay these taxes? The solution is in the document. A beneficiary might pay them and the successor trustee will reimburse that beneficiary.

A better solution might be to use insurance proceeds to pay those taxes, thereby providing the estate with needed liquidity.

> Upon the death of the Trustor, William Hook, or of any other beneficiary, any estate, inheritance, succession, or other death taxes, duties, charges or assessments, together with interest, penalties, costs, Trustee's compensation, and attorney's fees which shall become due by reason of the trust estate or any interest therein being includable in the Estate of the Trustor, or of such other beneficiary, for such tax purposes, may be paid from the trust estate by the Trustee, in its sole discretion, unless other adequate provision

shall have been made therefore. Any such payments shall be charged to the principal of the trust estate. The Trustee may make such payments directly, or to the Executory or other fiduciary of the Trustor or such other beneficiary, and may rely upon the written statement of such fiduciary as to the amount and propriety of such taxes, interest, penalties, and other costs. The decision of the Trustee as to any such payments shall be conclusive and binding upon all parties interested in this Trust or such Estate. If the trust estate shall be then insufficient or if it be then terminated the Trustee shall be reimbursed by the persons to whom the trust estate shall have been distributed, to the extent of the amount received by each distributee. The Trustee, before making any distribution of either income or principal, may accordingly require a refunding agreement or may withhold distribution pending determination or release of any tax lien.

The Trustee is authorized to acquire by purchase, exchange, or otherwise, property, real, personal, or mixed, from the Executor or Administrator of the Estate of any beneficiary of this Trust, even though such property may not be of a character prescribed by law or by the terms of the Trust instrument for the investment of Trust funds, and although the acquisition of such property may result in a large percentage or all of the trust estate being invested in one class of property. The Trustee is expressly authorized to retain the property so acquired so long as it shall deem this advisable and to make secured or unsecured loans to the Executor or Administrator of such Estate upon such terms as the Trustee shall deem advisable, such procedures being authorized to the extent that they do not adversely affect or diminish the marital deduction available to the Estate. Such purchases or loans shall be without liability to the Trustee for loss resulting to the trust estate therefrom. In any dealings with a fiduciary of the Estate, the Trustee may rely upon the statement of such fiduciary as to all material facts.

Any portion of the trust estate which was received from any qualified plan as described in Section 2039 of the Internal Revenue Code of 1954, as amended, or any subsequent like or similar law, may not be used for any purpose described in this Article, which would result in the inclusion of said funds in the taxable Federal Estate of the Trustor so long as other sources of funds are available.

If the Trustee considers/consider that any distribution from a Trust hereunder other than pursuant to a power to withdraw or appoint is a taxable distribution subject to a generation-skipping tax payable by the distributee, the Trustee shall augment the distribution by an amount which the Trustee estimates/estimate to be sufficient to pay the tax and shall charge the same against the Trust to which the tax relates. If the Trustee considers that any termination of an interest in or power over Trust property hereunder is a taxable termination subject to a generation-skipping tax, the Trustee shall pay the tax from the Trust property to which the tax relates, without adjustment of the relative interests of the beneficiaries. If the tax is imposed in part by reason of the Trust property hereunder and in part by reason of other property, the Trustee shall pay that portion thereof which the value of the Trust property bears to the total property taxed, taking into consideration deductions, exemptions, and other factors which the Trustee deems pertinent.

## Payment of Trust Expenses

All estates will have various ongoing expenses after a death. These expenses can be simple, as in cleaning up outstanding bills. Or complex as in keeping a mortgage current, taxes paid, and special distributions on schedule. As herein provided, the Trustee has the power to pay any and all bills and expenses associated with the management of the estate.

The Trustee shall have the authority to pay all costs, charges, and expenses of the trust estate, together with reasonable compensation for the Trustee's services hereunder, including services in whole or partial distribution of the trust estate; and to employ and compensate from the trust estate such agents, assistants, and attorneys as in the Trustee's judgment shall be necessary to protect and manage the Trust property.

# Commence or Defend Litigation

Should there be a lawsuit against the trust, Mr. Hook has provided for a defense against a legal attack.

The Trustee may commence or defend such litigation with respect to the Trust or any property of the trust estate as the Trustee may deem advisable at the expense of the Trust.

# Compromise Claims

This clause gives the successor trustee the power to negotiate on behalf of the trust.

> The Trustee may compromise or otherwise adjust any claims or litigation against or in favor of the Trust.

# Adjust for Tax Consequences

This clause provides the power to manage the entire trust estate in a manner that will minimize any tax consequence and liability.

> The Trustee shall have the power, in the Trustee's absolute discretion, to take any action and to make any election to minimize the tax liabilities of this Trust and its beneficiaries and to allocate the benefits among the various beneficiaries and to make adjustments in the rights of any beneficiaries or between the income and the principal accounts, to compensate for the consequence of any tax election or any investment or administrative decision that the Trustee believes has had the effect of directly or indirectly preferring one beneficiary or group of beneficiaries over others.

# Budget Income and Expenses

As successor trustee, John has the right to manage any and all income.

> The Trustee shall have the power to budget the estimated annual income and expenses of the Trust or Trust share in such manner as to equalize as far as possible periodic income payments to beneficiaries.

The above basic clauses in the trust agreement will enable you, as surviving trustee, successor trustee, or successor co-trustee, to manage and settle the average trust estate. If you feel overwhelmed by the above clauses, you can always seek professional help.

In addition, there may be other enabling clauses that will provide power to the trustee or successor trustee that encompass different areas not covered here.

Other sections of the trust document not detailed here should include:

## DECLARATION OF TRUST

This is where the individual(s) who created the trust declare the purpose of the trust and include an identification of the parties to the trust.

## TRUST PROPERTY

Here you will find definitions of property type and nature of ownership.

## SETTLOR POWERS

These are the administrative powers granted to the creator(s) or "settlor(s)" of the trust.

# Management of a Married Trust

If the decedent was married, the entire trust estate may not be settled immediately. It would be managed or administered by or for the benefit of the decedent's surviving spouse until the passing of that person.

# Survivor's Trust A

The following clauses—Right to Income, Right to Principal, Right to Withdraw Principal, Control of Assets, Right to Change Beneficiary, and Distribution of Residual of Trust A—set forth the rights afforded the decedent's surviving spouse under the survivor's Trust A section of an A married, A-B, or A-B-C revocable living trust.

Upon or after the death of a Settlor, the Trustee(s) shall hold, administer, and distribute the trust estate as follows:

## RIGHT TO INCOME

The survivor's Trust A holds the assets allocated to the surviving spouse. These assets "belong" to the surviving spouse, who has absolute control over those assets placed into this trust division.

Commencing with the date of predeceased Spouse's death, the Trustee(s) shall pay to or apply for the benefit of the surviving Spouse, during his or her lifetime, all the net income from the trust estate in convenient installments but no less frequently than quarterly.

## RIGHT TO PRINCIPAL

Since the assets are under complete control of the surviving spouse, he or she has the right to spend that trust estate on whatever he or she desires. The surviving spouse may even spend the entire amount of these funds.

In addition, the Trustee(s) may pay to or apply for the benefit of the surviving Spouse such sums from the principal of Trust A as in their sole discretion shall be necessary or advisable from time to time for the medical care, comfortable maintenance, and welfare of the surviving Spouse, taking into consideration to the extent the Trustee(s) deem(s) advisable any other income or resources of the surviving Spouse known to the Trustee(s).

## RIGHT TO WITHDRAW PRINCIPAL

The surviving spouse may remove all of the assets in Trust A if that spouse wishes. This would effectively "de-fund" the trust and remove the protection afforded to those assets by the trust. As long as the surviving spouse is the trustee of Trust A, no written notice is needed to execute any action that affects the assets held in the trust estate.

The surviving Spouse may, at any time during his or her lifetime and from time to time, withdraw all or any part of the principal of the trust estate, free of Trust, by delivering to the Trustee(s) an instrument in writing, duly signed by the surviving Spouse, describing the property or portion thereof desired to be withdrawn. Upon receipt of such instrument, the Trustee(s) shall thereupon convey and deliver to the surviving Spouse, free of Trust, the property described in such instrument.

## CONTROL OF ASSETS

The surviving spouse retains the same control over the assets in the trust as if he or she "owned" those assets in their individual name. He or she may make any investment decision free of encumbrance by other parties. Again, as long as the surviving spouse is the trustee of Trust A, no written notice is needed.

The surviving Spouse may, at any time by written notice, require the Trustee(s) either to make any nonproductive property of this Trust productive or to convert productive property to nonproductive property, each within a reasonable time. The surviving Spouse may further require the Trustee(s) to invest part, or all, of this share of Trust assets for the purpose of maximizing income rather than growth, or growth rather than income.

## RIGHT TO CHANGE BENEFICIARY

Under the provisions of an A married revocable living trust, the surviving spouse, if that person is the trustee, retains the right to remove or add beneficiaries as he or she wishes. Even after the passing of the first spouse, the Trust A remains revocable, and therefore changeable by the surviving spouse.

The surviving Spouse retains the right to change the beneficiaries of this Trust.

## DISTRIBUTION OF RESIDUAL OF TRUST A

The surviving spouse can change the allocation and distribution to the beneficiaries of the trust. This means that while he or she is the trustee of the trust, changes can be made that impact upon who are the heirs, what they are to receive, and when they are to receive their share or specific asset(s).

Husband or wife, as an original trustee, has the absolute right to spend every last dime on whatever and however he or she chooses. The trust is for their benefit while he or she is living. Residual distribution means exactly that. The successor trustee(s) is going to distribute to the beneficiaries (heirs) only that which remains in the trust estate after the passing of the surviving spouse.

> After the death of the Settlors, the balance of the principal shall be distributed in accordance with the provisions specified in the section of this Trust titled *Allocation and Distribution.*

# Administration of Trust Estates Using an A-B or A-B-C Living Trust

These trusts, used by a married couple, include provisions for splitting the trust into separate parts. This would be done for the following reasons:

1. In order to take advantage of both husband's and wife's $600,000 personal estate exemptions, thereby shielding their estate from all federal inheritance taxes up to $1,200,000 of estate net value.

2. If in the case of a second marriage, the husband and wife had different primary beneficiaries and each wanted to make sure that their respective beneficiaries received their inheritance.

# Decedent's Trust B

If the decedent's estate was held in trust using an A married or single form of living trust, disregard this section completely.

The following clauses—Payment of Income, Payment of Principal, Discretionary Payments, Control of Assets, and Distribution of Residual of Trust B—set forth the rights afforded the surviving spouse under the decedent's Trust B section of an A-B or A-B-C revocable living trust.

Decedent's Trust B shall be irrevocable and shall be held, administered, and distributed as follows:

## PAYMENT OF INCOME

The decedent's Trust B holds the assets allocated to the deceased spouse. These assets "belong" to Trust B. Upon the passing of the first spouse, this trust becomes *irrevocable*. The surviving spouse cannot change the allocation or distribution to the beneficiaries of the deceased spouse. The surviving spouse does have certain rights associated with this division, one of which is the right to receive all the income generated by the assets in Trust B. This income must be used to maintain his or her standard of living and general well-being.

> Commencing with the date of deceased Spouse's death, the Trustee(s) shall pay to or apply for the benefit of the surviving Spouse during his or her lifetime all the net income from Trust B in convenient installments but no less frequently than quarterly.

## PAYMENT OF PRINCIPAL

In addition to the above right of the surviving spouse to receive all the income to Trust B, he or she has a right to access the principal as well.

If the income generated by the assets in Trust B is insufficient to maintain the "standard of living" and "well-being" of the surviving spouse, he or she has the right to spend the principal of this division. These funds are to be spent in maintaining the surviving spouse's "standard of living." The question you as the surviving spouse and/or trustee might be asking is, Who determines that standard of living? It is the surviving spouse. He or she can spend the entire Trust B estate providing for the same standard of living that the surviving spouse enjoyed when both husband and wife were living.

> The Trustee(s) may pay to, or apply for the benefit of, the surviving Spouse, during his or her lifetime, such sums from the principal of Trust B as in the Trustees' sole discretion shall be

necessary or advisable from time to time for the medical care, education, and maintenance of the surviving Spouse, taking into consideration to the extent the Trustee deems advisable any other income or resources of the surviving Spouse known to the Trustee(s).

## DISCRETIONARY PAYMENTS

This is the third right to obtain income from the decedent's Trust B. It is referred to as the "frivolous right." The surviving spouse has a right to spend a predetermined amount in any fashion he or she wants. Unlike the other two rights above, there are no restrictions placed on how these funds may be spent.

In addition to the income and discretionary payments of principal from this Trust, there shall be paid to the surviving Spouse, during his or her lifetime, from the principal of this Trust, upon the surviving Spouse's written request, during the last month of each fiscal year of the Trust an amount not to exceed during such fiscal year the amount of five thousand ($5,000) dollars or five percent (5%) of the aggregate value of principal for such fiscal year, whichever year, whichever is greater. This right of withdrawal is noncumulative, so that if the surviving Spouse does not withdraw, during such fiscal year, the full amount to which he or she is entitled under this Paragraph, his or her right to withdraw the amount not withdrawn shall lapse at the end of that fiscal year.

## CONTROL OF ASSETS

Even though the decedent's Trust B is irrevocable, if the surviving spouse is designated trustee, the trust can provide for the spouse to retain active management control over the nature of the assets.

> The surviving Spouse may, at any time by written notice, require the Trustee(s) either to make any nonproductive property of this Trust productive or to convert productive to non-productive property, each within a reasonable time. The surviving Spouse may further require the Trustee(s) to invest part, or all, of this share of Trust assets for the purpose of maximizing income rather than growth, or growth rather than income.

## DISTRIBUTION OF RESIDUAL OF DECEDENT'S TRUST B

The surviving spouse cannot change the allocation and distribution to the beneficiaries of Trust B. This means that while he or she is the trustee of this trust, *no* changes can be made that impact anyone who is an heir of this trust, what they are to receive, and when they are to receive their share or specific asset(s) from this trust.

Residual distribution means exactly that. The successor trustee(s) is/are going to distribute to the decedent's beneficiaries (heirs) only what remains in the trust estate after the passing of the surviving spouse.

The balance of the principal of Trust B shall be distributed in accordance with the provisions specified in the section of this Trust titled Allocation and Distribution.

If the Spouse, whose share is represented by this Trust B, makes specific provision for beneficiaries, allocation, and distribution, and such provision cannot be complied with due to the death of a specified beneficiary, or if for any reason a specified distribution cannot be made as directed, then provisions of Per Stirpes, Intestate Succession, and Charity as specified herein shall govern distribution, with reference to the affected Settlor's beneficiaries and share.

# Decedent's Trust C

If the decedent's estate was held in an A married or A-B married form of revocable living trust, disregard this section completely.

The following clauses—Payment of Income, Payment of Principal, Control of Assets, and Distribution of Residual of Trust C—set forth the rights afforded the surviving spouse under the decedent's Trust C section of an A-B-C (QTIP) married revocable living trust (Qualified Terminable Interest Property Trust).

Decedent's Trust C shall be irrevocable and shall be held, administered, and distributed as follows:

## PAYMENT OF INCOME

The decedent's Trust C holds the assets allocated to the deceased spouse that are valued in excess of the deceased spouse's $600,000 personal estate exemption. These assets "belong" to Trust C. Upon the passing of the first spouse, this trust became *irrevocable*. The surviving spouse cannot change the allocation or distribution to the beneficiaries of the deceased spouse. The surviving spouse does have certain rights associated with Trust C, one of which is the right to receive all the income generated by the assets in the trust. This income is to be used to maintain his or her standard of living and general well-being.

Commencing with the date of Predeceased Spouse's death, the Trustee shall pay to or apply for the benefit of the surviving Spouse during his or her lifetime all the net income from Trust C in convenient installments but no less frequently than quarterly.

## PAYMENT OF PRINCIPAL

In addition to the above right of the surviving spouse to receive all the income to Trust C, he or she has a right to access the principal as well.

If the income generated by the assets in Trusts B and

C are insufficient to maintain the "standard of living" and "well-being" of the surviving spouse, he or she has the right to spend the principal of this division C. These funds are to be spent in maintaining the surviving spouse's "standard of living." Again, the surviving spouse determines that standard of living. He or she can spend the entire C Trust estate providing for the same standard of living and lifestyle that the surviving spouse enjoyed when both husband and wife were living.

> The Trustee may pay to, or apply for the benefit of, the surviving Spouse, during his or her lifetime, such sums from the principal of Trust C as in the Trustee's sole discretion shall be necessary or advisable from time to time for the medical care, education, and maintenance of the surviving Spouse, taking into consideration to the extent the Trustee deems advisable any other income or resources of the surviving Spouse known to the Trustee.

## CONTROL OF ASSETS

Again, even though the decedent's Trust C is irrevocable, the surviving spouse, if trustee, can still have active management control over the nature of the assets in this trust if provided for.

> The surviving Spouse may, at any time by written notice, require the Trustee either to make any nonproductive property of this trust productive or to convert productive property to

nonproductive property, each within a reasonable time. The surviving Spouse may further require the Trustee to invest part, or all, of this share of Trust assets for the purpose of maximizing income rather than growth, or growth rather than income.

## DISTRIBUTION OF RESIDUAL OF TRUST C

The surviving spouse cannot change the allocation and distribution to the beneficiaries of Trust C. This means that while he or she is the trustee of this trust, *no* changes can be made that impact who is an heir of this trust, what they are to receive, and when they are to receive their share or specific assets(s) from this trust.

Residual distribution means exactly that. After the payment of inheritance, estate, or other taxes and expenses have been made, the successor trustee(s) is/are going to distribute to the named beneficiaries (heirs) only that which remains in the trust estate after the passing of the surviving spouse.

Upon the death of the surviving Settlor, the balance of Trust C shall be distributed as specified in "Distribution of Residual of Trust C" as constituted on the date of death of the first of the Settlors to die, giving effect to the original provisions of the Trust agreement and any amendments thereto then in existence.

If the Spouse whose share is represented by this Trust C makes specific provision for beneficiaries, allocation, and distribution, and such provision cannot be complied with due to the death of a specified beneficiary, or if for any reason a specified distribution cannot be made as directed, then provisions of Per Stirpes, Intestate Succession, and Charity as specified herein shall govern distribution, with reference to the affected Settlor's beneficiaries and share.

## But Is All This Worth It?

You might be saying to yourself, "Gee, all these clauses and sections seem really confusing." It may appear complicated, but it is in fact simpler. A properly drawn living trust is by far a much more comprehensive document than the typical last will and testament. It has to be. It is the center of authority for all powers vested through it. Please remember that the more detailed the document, the more power you as a surviving or successor trustee will have and the more contingencies will be covered. Little is left to the imagination of others or assumed.

# A Word About "Micro-Management"

There could be pages of detailed instructions on how the surviving or successor trustee(s) is to handle every detail for the management of trust estate assets. Some people, after death, want to have the ability to "micro-manage" the estates they left behind. This rarely works to the benefit of the estate and its beneficiaries, as the following example will show. I knew of a gentleman who had become a millionaire by investing in real estate. Over the years, he purchased, leveraged, traded, and exchanged a variety of properties. At the time of his passing, he owned nineteen commercial buildings along a very busy and popular boulevard. All of these buildings were filled with paying tenants.

When this gentleman died in 1990, real estate was a hot ticket in Los Angeles. It was a seller's market, with properties being snapped up by buyers at a feverish pace. In the trustee powers section of his living trust document, he forbade his successor trustee to sell any property for a period of five years from the date of his death. He was told that it was unwise to place such a restriction on the ability of his successor trustee to manage the affairs of his trust, but he was adamant that this instruction be added to his trust.

It has now been six years since he died. Southern California has experienced a devastating and lingering economic downturn. Some experts have even called it a depression. Real estate suffered terribly, as have many small shop and business owners. The portfolio of properties in this trust has taken a major financial beating. Seven properties sit vacant because the tenant's businesses failed and new tenants cannot be found. Of the nine buildings that still have a paying tenant, all have renegotiated their rents downward and many pay late. Income is effectively half of what it was in 1990.

Three properties have gone "back to the bank." The average appraised value of the remaining sixteen buildings is 37 percent less than their value in 1990! And the buyers? They're nowhere to be found.

This is the kind of damage that micro-management can inadvertently inflict upon an estate and the loved ones left behind.

# Dealing with the Tax Man

Please review *"Step 7. Prepare All Tax Returns."* The calculation and payment of taxes are a function of estate settlement no matter the form it takes. As the old saying goes, "Nothing in life is certain but death and taxes." Taxes are with us all our lives and can even accompany us into the great hereafter.

A major estate settlement process concerns the payment of taxes. Upon the decedent's passing, the federal government, as well as some state governments, will want their "fair share" of everything he or she left behind. On large estates, Uncles Sam's "fair share" can be as high as 55 percent of the estate's assets!

# FEDERAL ESTATE TAXES

The federal inheritance tax rate starts at the same rate as the federal gift tax. It is a very confiscatory tax structure. Estate and gift taxes are levied in a manner much like that of income taxes. As the value of the estate increases, the tax brackets change and the percentage of levied taxes increases.

For example, if a person (without a spouse) dies and leaves an estate of $1,000,000, you may conclude that he or she died a millionaire and that it will all be put to good use for the benefit of the family. But Uncle Sam is going to say, "Wait a minute! On that taxable million the decedent has a unified credit of $600,000 [see below]; of the $400,000 taxable dollars left, there is a graduated tax of 37 to 39 percent." Plus, he'll take 41 percent of every dollar between $1,000,000 and $1,250,000.

## THE UNIFIED CREDIT

Each person has a unified credit that will reduce the amount of estate tax that may have to be paid. It is equivalent to having $600,000 worth of assets which are not subject to the federal inheritance tax. The amount is $1,200,000 for a married couple using an A-B or A-B-C (QTIP) living trust.

## ESTATE TAX CALCULATOR

The following tax calculator may be used as a general guide for answering two important questions:

1. Will the estate be subject to federal inheritance tax?

# INHERITANCE TAX CALCULATOR

| AT TIME OF PASSING OF INDIVIDUAL OR FIRST SPOUSE AN ESTATE VALUED AT. NET VALUE | PERCENTAGE RATE BRACKETS FOR FEDERAL INHERITANCE TAX. TAX PAID | SINGLE INDIVIDUAL WITHOUT USING A TRUST OR USING AN A SINGLE LIVING TRUST. TAX PAID | MARRIED COUPLE WITHOUT USING A TRUST OR USING AN A MARRIED LIVING TRUST. TAX PAID | MARRIED COUPLE USING AN AB MARRIED LIVING TRUST. TAX PAID |
|---|---|---|---|---|
| $600,000 | 37% | $0 | $0 | $0 |
| $625,000 | 37% | $9,250 | $9,250 | $0 |
| $650,000 | 37% | $18,500 | $18,500 | $0 |
| $700,000 | 37% | $37,000 | $37,000 | $0 |
| $750,000 | 37% | $55,500 | $55,500 | $0 |
| $800,000 | 39% | $75,000 | $75,000 | $0 |
| $850,000 | 39% | $94,500 | $94,500 | $0 |
| $900,000 | 39% | $114,000 | $114,000 | $0 |
| $1,000,000 | 39% | $153,000 | $153,000 | $0 |
| $1,100,000 | 41% | $194,000 | $194,000 | $0 |
| $1,200,000 | 41% | $235,000 | $235,000 | $0 |
| $1,300,000 | 43% | $277,000 | $277,000 | $42,000 |
| $1,400,000 | 43% | $320,000 | $320,000 | $85,000 |
| $1,500,000 | 43% | $363,000 | $363,000 | $128,000 |
| $1,600,000 | 45% | $408,000 | $408,000 | $173,000 |
| $1,700,000 | 45% | $453,000 | $453,000 | $218,000 |
| $1,800,000 | 45% | $498,000 | $498,000 | $263,000 |
| $1,900,000 | 45% | $543,000 | $543,000 | $308,000 |
| $2,000,000 | 45% | $588,000 | $588,000 | $353,000 |
| $3,000,000 | 50% * | $1,275,000 | $1,275,000 | $889,000 |
| $5,000,000 | 50% * | $2,275,000 | $2,275,000 | $1,889,000 |
| $10,000,000 | 55% * ** | $4,948,000 | $4,948,000 | $4,713,000 |

2. If this tax has to be paid, how much will it be?

This calculator is based on the assumption that no unified credit has been used by the decedent prior to the individual's passing. It should not be substituted for more detailed accounting procedures.

This calculator does not reflect any state and local taxes that may be levied against the estate.

The Budget Reconciliation Act of 1993 lowered the rates from 53 percent, 55 percent, and 60 percent respectively, but are subject to a 5 percent surcharge on assets exceeding $10,000,000 until the benefits of the unified credit and the lower graduated tax brackets have been recaptured. In other words, until the entire taxable estate is taxed at a flat 55 percent.

If the decedent had an estate of $3,000,000 at the time of his or her passing, Uncle Sam is going to take $1,290,800 plus 55 percent of everything over $3,000,000.

## FEDERAL "TAX BREAKS"

If you are a surviving spouse, there are two tax exemptions you should be aware of that are known as "tax breaks."

The first tax exemption is the *unlimited marital* deduction, which benefits only married couples. It's a simple, easy-to-understand situation. If the decedent was married at the time of his or her passing, they could simply "gift" *all* of their assets, the entire estate, to the surviving spouse free of any federal inheritance or gift taxes. There is no limit as to the size of the estate—it can be $1,000,000,000 and there will still be no inheritance taxes levied by Uncle Sam.

There are two major problems with married couples

using this "tax break." First, when the surviving spouse passes away, the estate could be hit with heavy federal inheritance taxes. In an estate over $3,000,000, this could be as high as 55 percent. Second, probate codes may circumvent the ability of the decedent to "gift" the entire estate to the surviving spouse. Please review Appendix I for state-by-state general guidelines in your particular situation. If you have questions concerning the estate's ability to forgo the payment of federal inheritance taxes, please consult your accountant, attorney, or the IRS directly.

The other inheritance "tax break" applies to everyone whether single, married, widowed, or divorced. It's called the *personal estate exemption* and we all have it automatically: if at the time of the decedent's passing, the *net value* of all of the assets in the estate is less than $600,000, there will be no federal inheritance taxes. Keep in mind that Uncle Sam includes everything the decedent owned when determining the net value of his or her estate. This includes property, securities, art, furniture, jewelry, even the face value of life insurance policies.

But there is a catch that you, as the person in charge of settling the estate, should be aware of. When a husband passes away, $600,000 will be exempt from federal inheritance taxes, and when his wife passes away, another $600,000 *can* or *cannot* be exempt. Unless the property was held in an A-B (bypass) or A-B-C (QTIP) trust, only *one* $600,000 exemption can be claimed.

Through an A-B (bypass) or A-B-C (QTIP) living trust, a married couple can combine each of their federal $600,000 personal estate exemptions. This will shield the estate from federal inheritance taxes up to

$1,200,000. The value of this tax protection alone can be worth over $185,000 to the surviving family.

## INCOME TAXES (CAPITAL GAINS)

Whether the decedent had a last will and testament or a living trust, he or she will receive a death benefit on capital assets. If he or she did not own that asset jointly with another, that person will obtain a 100 percent "stepped-up basis" or "stepped-up valuation" on any and all owned capital assets: real estate, stocks, etc. The original cost (basis) of the asset will get "stepped up" or changed to the market value (sales price) of that asset as of the date the owner passed away. Since the cost (basis) is now the same as the market value (sales price), there is no more gain, and no income or capital gain tax to be paid on the proceeds from the sale of the asset.

For a more in-depth explanation, please review the section on joint ownership for information on the determination if any taxes are due and calculation of this form of federal tax.

## STATE ESTATE TAXES

Some states will have the authority to levy and collect an "estate" tax upon the decedent's estate. This tax is in addition to or in lieu of any federal "inheritance" tax. The estate tax levy is different in every state imposing this form of tax. The laws, codes, and regulations governing such taxation change frequently. Contact a local source in the state of residence and other states where the decedent owned property to obtain specific threshold, rate, and exemption information that applies to your particular situation. An accountant should be a good source for this information.

In states classified as "federal credit," "federal exempt," or "pick up," there are no additional estate taxes over and above those paid to the federal government upon the passing of an individual.

Twenty-seven states come under this *tax-exempt* status: Alabama, Alaska, Arizona, Arkansas, California, Colorado, Florida, Georgia, Hawaii, Idaho, Illinois, Maine, Minnesota, Missouri, Montana, Nevada, New Hampshire, New Mexico, North Dakota, Oregon, Texas, Utah, Vermont, Virginia, Washington, West Virginia, and Wyoming.

The other twenty-three states levy an estate tax upon a passing. This is in addition to any federal inheritance tax that might be due. The *tax-collecting* states are: Connecticut, Delaware, Indiana, Iowa, Kansas, Kentucky, Louisiana, Maryland, Massachusetts, Michigan, Mississippi, Nebraska, New Jersey, New York, North Carolina, Ohio, Oklahoma, Pennsylvania, Rhode Island, South Carolina, South Dakota, Tennessee, and Wisconsin.

## STATE ESTATE INCOME TAXES

In addition, most states can set an income tax on the estate. Since probate is a lengthy process, the decedent's affairs cannot be wrapped up quickly to help mitigate the impact of this tax upon the estate. As income flows into the estate from various sources—a business, investment income, dividends, etc.—it might be considered as ordinary income to the estate and taxed as such. The executor, executrix, administrator, or personal representative is responsible to see to it that this tax is calculated and paid. It will have to be paid prior to any estate distribution. It may need to be paid to the probate court, which in turn will forward it to the proper taxing authority.

Each state that imposes such a tax will have a tax threshold below which no taxes will be due. In addition, the rates on such taxes change with some regularity, so it would be wise to check with a local source of information about your own particular situation.

## STATE INHERITANCE TAX

The state may also require that an heir or beneficiary pay a tax on the value of their inheritance. The amount of such taxes usually is determined by the relationship of the heir to the decedent. The closer the relationship, the lower the tax, so that a wife, son, or daughter of the decedent will be required to pay a smaller tax than a brother or sister of the decedent.

The following list will show you which twenty states *DO* and which thirty *DO NOT* impose a state inheritance tax on the heirs or beneficiaries.

These twenty states *DO* charge the heirs an inheritance tax: Connecticut, Delaware, Indiana, Iowa, Kansas, Kentucky, Louisiana, Maryland, Michigan, Montana, Nebraska, New Hampshire, New Jersey, North Carolina, Pennsylvania, South Dakota, Tennessee, Texas, West Virginia, Wisconsin.

These thirty states *DO NOT* charge the heirs an inheritance tax: Alabama, Alaska, Arizona, Arkansas, California, Colorado, Florida, Georgia, Hawaii, Idaho, Illinois, Maine, Massachusetts, Minnesota, Mississippi, Missouri, Nevada, New Mexico, New York, North Dakota, Ohio, Oklahoma, Oregon, Rhode Island, South Carolina, Utah, Vermont, Virginia, Washington, Wyoming.

# Appendix I
# Probate State by State:
# Rules, Fees, and Rights

The following is a brief outline of the probate process in each of the fifty states. The information for each state outline is divided into specific sections that include:

*Competent Jurisdiction*

Where the laws governing the process will be found along with areas of competent court jurisdiction.

*Will Proving Methods*

What methods are used and accepted for determining the validity of the last will and testament presented to the court.

*Forms of Administration*

Which estates need to be probated and what form that process will take.

*Out-of-State Personal Representative, Executor, Executrix*

The ability to have a nonresident handle the probate process and his or her fee schedule.

### Court-Appointed Administrator

Who can be appointed by the court to handle the estate, and the fees that can be charged.

### Estimated Attorney Fees

What and/or how a lawyer hired to represent the estate can charge the estate for those services.

### Asset Inventory and Property Appraisal

What form and supervision will be required?

### Creditors' Claim Window

What form and supervision will be required?

### Joint Property Ownership

How is co-owned property held?

### Spousal Shares and Rights

AUTOMATIC: What can the surviving spouse receive without question?

INTESTATE: What can the surviving spouse receive if the decedent leaves no will?

RIGHT OF ELECTION: What is the absolute minimum a surviving spouse can claim under a last will and testament?

# Alabama

## Competent Jurisdiction

Probate Court, state codes, county by county.

## Will Proving Methods

FORMAL: Testimony of one witness establishing hand-writing (signature) of deceased and/or testimony of one signing witness.

SELF-PROVING: Sanctioned.

## Forms of Administration

SUPERVISED: For all estates.

SUMMARY: Not automatic, relative of decedent must petition for summary and allowed only where estate does not exceed $3,000 in personal property after all claims and debts paid.

## Out-of-State Personal Representative, Executor, Executrix

Non-Alabama resident allowed if named in proved will.

FEES: 2.5 percent of all income, value of personal property and debt service. Court can provide for higher percentage.

## Court-Appointed Administrator

Court-appointed must be Alabama resident.

FEES: Same as personal representative.

### Estimated Attorney Fees

Set by court. Extraordinary fees okay.

### Asset Inventory and Property Appraisal

Must start within two months of confirmation of personal representative or appointment of administrator. Private appraiser at court approval.

### Creditors' Claim Window

Open: six months after confirmation of personal representative or appointment of administrator.

### Joint Property Ownership

Joint tenants, tenants in common, and tenants by entirety okay. Tenants in common assumed. Joint tenants must be stated.

### Spousal Shares and Rights

AUTOMATIC: Homestead up to $6,000. Personal property up to $3,500. All family expenses during probate (up to one year).

INTESTATE: Entire estate if no living parent. Or $100,000 + half of remainder if one living parent but no issue. Or $50,000 + half of remainder if living issue are all surviving spouse's issue. Or half of entire estate if one or more than one living issue are not issue of surviving spouse.

RIGHT OF ELECTION: One-third of entire estate. Or entire estate (minus spouse's sole and separate property), whichever is the lesser of the two. Spouse must elect within six months of decedent's death or six months from proof of will, whichever is later.

# ALASKA

*Competent Jurisdiction*

Superior Court, state statutes, county by county.

## Will Proving Methods

FORMAL: Testimony of one signing witness or by one witness establishing evidence of authenticity.

INFORMAL: Testimony or affidavit of anyone with evidence of execution.

CONTESTED: Testimony of one signing witness.

SELF-PROVING: Sanctioned.

## Forms of Administration

SUPERVISED: Only upon petition from interested party. Range of control from full to minimal accounting or as required by court.

UNSUPERVISED: For all estates except where supervised petition accepted by court.

SUMMARY: If total estate, excluding real property claims, is less than spouse's marital exemption added to administration costs.

AFFIDAVIT: If total estate, excluding real property claims, is less than $15,000 + thirty-day wait + no pending personal representative application to the court.

## Out-of-State Personal Representative, Executor, Executrix

Non-Alaska allowed.

FEES: "Reasonable."

*Court-Appointed Administrator*

Non-Alaska allowed.

FEES: Same as personal representative.

*Estimated Attorney Fees*

"Reasonable."

*Asset Inventory and Property Appraisal*

Must start within three months of confirmation of personal representative or appointment of administrator. Private appraiser at court approval.

*Creditors' Claim Window*

Open: four months after first notice. If no notice, then three years from court-determined event.

*Joint Property Ownership*

Tenants in common if not married. Married holds as tenants by entirety unless stated otherwise. No joint tenant ownership of personal property.

*Spousal Shares and Rights*

AUTOMATIC: Homestead up to $27,000. Personal property up to $10,000 + "reasonable" family expenses up to one year.

INTESTATE: Entire estate if no living issue or parent. Or $50,000 + half of remainder if one living parent but no issue. Or half of entire estate if one or more than one living issue are not issue of surviving spouse.

RIGHT OF ELECTION:   One-third of entire estate. Spouse must elect within nine months of decedent's death or six months from proof of will, whichever is later.

# ARIZONA

*Competent Jurisdiction*

Superior Court, state statutes, county by county.

*Last Will and Testament Proving Methods*

FORMAL: Testimony of one signing witness or by one witness establishing evidence of authenticity.

INFORMAL: Testimony or affidavit of anyone with evidence of execution.

CONTESTED: Testimony of one signing witness.

SELF-PROVING: Sanctioned.

*Forms of Administration*

SUPERVISED: Only by petition from interested party. Range of control from full to minimal accounting or as required by court.

UNSUPERVISED: For all estates except where supervised petition accepted by court.

SUMMARY: If total estate (excluding real property claims) is less than spouse's marital exemption added to administration costs.

AFFIDAVIT: If total estate (including real property claims) is less than $15,000 + 180-day wait + no pending personal representative application to the court + all taxes, unsecured debt, administration, last illness, and funeral costs paid. Or if personal property only and all valued at $30,000 or less + all debts paid + thirty-day wait + no pending personal representative applica-

154

tion to the court. Or any estate with a value less than $5,000.

### Out-of-State Personal Representative, Executor, Executrix

Non-Arizona allowed.

FEES:   "Reasonable" fees.

### Court-Appointed Administrator

Non-Arizona allowed.

FEES:   Same as personal representative.

### Estimated Attorney Fees

"Reasonable" fees. Extraordinary fees okay.

### Asset Inventory and Property Appraisal

Must start within three months of confirmation of personal representative or appointment of administrator. Private appraiser at court approval.

### Creditors' Claim Window

Open: four months after first notice.

### Joint Property Ownership

Community property in Arizona. Property acquired in other state during marriage is quasi-community property under jurisdiction of Arizona law. Joint tenants must be stated. No tenants by entirety.

## Spousal Shares and Rights

AUTOMATIC:   Half of all community property + homestead up to $12,000 + personal property up to $7,000 + "reasonable" family expenses during probate.

INTESTATE:   Entire estate if no living issue or all living issue are spouse's. Or half of deceased spouse's separate property, but none of said spouse's half of community property if one or more than one living issue are not surviving spouse's.

RIGHT OF ELECTION:   None.

# ARKANSAS

## Competent Jurisdiction

Probate Court, state codes, county by county.

## Last Will and Testament Proving Methods

FORMAL: By two signing witnesses or testimony of one witness establishing handwriting (signature) of deceased and one signing witness.

SELF-PROVING: Sanctioned.

## Forms of Administration

SUPERVISED: For all estates.

SUMMARY: All estates under $50,000, after debts paid, and spousal election and/or rights taken + no personal representative application + forty-five day wait.

## Out-of-State Personal Representative, Executor, Executrix

Non-Arkansas resident allowed if named in proved will.

FEES: Set by court. 10 percent on first $1,000 of personal property + 5 percent on next $4,000 + 3 percent on remainder of personal property + "reasonable" fees if estate has real property.

## Court-Appointed Administrator

Court-appointed may be non-Arkansas resident.

FEES: Same as personal representative.

## Estimated Attorney Fees

Set by court. 5 percent of first $5,000 of any property + 4 percent of next $20,000 + 3 percent of next $75,000 + 2.75 percent of next $300,000 + 2.5 percent of next $600,000 + 2 percent of remainder. Extraordinary fees above court schedule okay.

## Asset Inventory and Property Appraisal

Must start within two months of confirmation of personal representative or appointment of administrator. Private appraiser at court approval.

## Creditors' Claim Window

Open: three months after first notice. If no notice, five years after decedent's death.

## Joint Property Ownership

Community property in Arkansas. Property acquired in other state during marriage also community property, if same in other state. Joint tenants and tenants in common must be stated. No tenants by entirety.

## Spousal Shares and Rights

AUTOMATIC: Half community property + homestead up to $2,500 + $1,000 value of personal property before creditors or $2,000 before all others + household furnishings deemed "necessary" by court + family expenses up to $500 per month for two months.

INTESTATE: Entire estate if married to decedent for more then three years and no living issue. Or half of estate if married to decedent less than three years and no living issue. Or nothing if living issue of decedent.

RIGHT OF ELECTION:   One-third of real property + one-third of personal property owned by decedent during marriage if married over one year and has living issue. Or half of entire estate before any other heirs or one-third before any creditors if no living issue. Or life estate in half, real property before any heirs or one-third before creditors and half of all personal property if real property in family for two generations. Spouse must elect within one month of creditor filing deadline or one month after litigation, if any, ends.

# California

## Competent Jurisdiction

Superior Court (Probate Division), state codes, county by county.

## Last Will and Testament Proving Methods

UNCONTESTED: By one signing witness, if unavailable by affidavit.

CONTESTED: Testimony of two signing witnesses or proof establishing execution.

SELF-PROVING: Allowed.

## Forms of Administration

SUPERVISED: For petitioned estates at or above $60,000 in personal property and/or $10,000 in real property.

SUMMARY: All estates under $60,000, excluding gifts to spouse, life insurance, and automobiles + no personal representative application + forty-day wait.

## Out-of-State Personal Representative, Executor, Executrix

Non-California resident allowed.

FEES: Set by court, 4 percent of first $15,000 + 3 percent of next $85,000 + 2 percent of next $900,000 + 1 percent of next $9,000,000 + .5 percent of next $15,000,000 + "reasonable" fees on remainder. Court can provide for higher fees. Extraordinary fees above court schedule okay.

### Court-Appointed Administrator

Court-appointed may be non-California resident.

FEES:   Same as personal representative.

### Estimated Attorney Fees

Same as personal representative. Extraordinary fees above court schedule okay.

### Asset Inventory and Property Appraisal

Must start within three months of confirmation of personal representative or appointment of administrator. Appraiser mandatory for all nonliquid assets. Private appraiser at court approval.

### Creditors' Claim Window

Open: one month after notice or four months after administrator appointment, whichever is longer.

### Joint Property Ownership

Community property in California. Property acquired in other state during marriage is quasi-community property, if same in other state. Joint tenants and tenants in common must be stated. No tenants by entirety.

### Spousal Shares and Rights

AUTOMATIC: One-half community property and quasi-community property and intestate share unless spouse waived rights in writing, specifically excluded in will or by property transfers before death + sixty-day use of home after filing inventory + "reasonable" family expenses determined by court.

INTESTATE:   Entire community property estate + half quasi-community property + half separate property of decedent if no living issue, living issue of issue, or living parent. Or one-third separate property if one living issue or one living issue and living issue of deceased or living issue of two deceased issue, or if no issue, all separate property.

RIGHT OF ELECTION:   None.

# COLORADO

## Competent Jurisdiction

District Court (Denver = Probate Court), state statutes, county by county.

## Last Will and Testament Proving Methods

FORMAL:   Testimony or affidavit of one signing witness or by establishing evidence of authenticity.

INFORMAL:   Testimony or affidavit of anyone with evidence of execution.

CONTESTED:   Testimony of one signing witness.

SELF-PROVING:   Sanctioned.

## Forms of Administration

SUPERVISED:   Upon petition from interested party. Range of control from full to minimal accounting or as required by court.

UNSUPERVISED:   For all estates except where supervised petition accepted by court.

SUMMARY:   If total estate, excluding real property claims, is less than spouse's marital exemption added to last illness, funeral, and probate costs.

AFFIDAVIT:   If total estate, including real property claims, is less than $20,000 + ten-day wait + no pending personal representative or heir application.

## Out-of-State Personal Representative, Executor, Executrix

Non-Colorado allowed.

FEES: "Reasonable" fees.

### Court-Appointed Administrator

Non-Colorado allowed.

FEES: Same as personal representative.

### Estimated Attorney Fees

"Reasonable" fees.

### Asset Inventory and Property Appraisal

Must start within three months of confirmation of personal representative or appointment of administrator. Private appraiser at court approval.

### Creditors' Claim Window

Open: four months after first notice or one year from date of decedent's death, whichever is earlier.

### Joint Property Ownership

Community property in Colorado. Property acquired in other state during marriage is quasi-community property under jurisdiction of Colorado law. Joint tenants must be stated. No tenants by entirety.

### Spousal Shares and Rights

AUTOMATIC: Half of all community property + personal property up to $7,500 + "reasonable" family expenses during probate up to one year.

INTESTATE: Entire estate if no living issue. Or $25,000 + half of remainder if living issue are all surviving spouse's issue. Or half of estate if one or more than one living issue are not surviving spouse's.

RIGHT OF ELECTION: Half of estate. Must elect within six months of first creditor notice or one year of decedent's death, whichever is earlier.

# CONNECTICUT

*Competent Jurisdiction*

Probate Court, state statutes, county by county.

*Last Will and Testament Proving Methods*

FORMAL:   By court ruling, case by case.

SELF-PROVING:   Sanctioned.

*Forms of Administration*

SUPERVISED:   For all estates.

SUMMARY:   Not automatic, relative of decedent must petition for summary and allowed only where estate does not exceed $20,000 in personal property after all claims and debts paid.

*Out-of-State Personal Representative, Executor, Executrix*

Non-Connecticut resident allowed if named in proved will + grants secretary of state power of attorney.

FEES:   "Reasonable" fees.

*Court-Appointed Administrator*

Court-appointed non-Connecticut + grants secretary of state power of attorney.

FEES:   Same as personal representative.

*Estimated Attorney Fees*

"Reasonable" fees. Extraordinary fees okay.

### Asset Inventory and Property Appraisal

Must start within two months of confirmation of personal representative or appointment of administrator. Private appraiser at court approval.

### Creditors' Claim Window

Open: three to twelve months of notice, set by court, case by case.

### Joint Property Ownership

Tenants in common presumed. Joint tenants must be stated. No tenants by entirety.

### Spousal Shares and Rights

AUTOMATIC: Living expenses set by court, case by case. Use of other assets set by court, case by case.

INTESTATE: Entire estate if no living parent. Or $25,000 + half of remainder if living issue are all surviving spouse's issue. Or half of entire estate if one or more than one living issue are not issue of surviving spouse.

RIGHT OF ELECTION: Half of entire estate. Spouse must elect within six months of first creditor notice or within one year of death, whichever is earlier.

# DELAWARE

## Competent Jurisdiction

Chancery (Registrar of Wills), state codes, county by county.

## Last Will and Testament Proving Methods

FORMAL:   Testimony of two signing witnesses or testimony and affidavit of one witness or testimony of one witness verifying decedent's signature.

SELF-PROVING:   Allowed.

## Forms of Administration

SUPERVISED:   For all estates.

SUMMARY:   Estates comprised of personal property valued at $12,500 or less + relative or personal representative application filed + thirty days since death of decedent.

## Out-of-State Personal Representative, Executor, Executrix

Non-Delaware resident allowed if named in proved will + grants registrar of wills power of attorney.

FEES:   Set by court.

## Court-Appointed Administrator

Court-appointed non-Delaware + sixty days + grants registrar of wills power of attorney.

FEES:   Same as personal representative.

*Estimated Attorney Fees*

Set by court. Extraordinary fees okay.

*Asset Inventory and Property Appraisal*

Must start within three months of confirmation of personal representative or appointment of administrator. Private appraiser at court approval.

*Creditors' Claim Window*

Open: eight months of decedent's death.

*Joint Property Ownership*

Tenants in common presumed, if married tenants by entirety. Joint tenants must be stated.

*Spousal Shares and Rights*

AUTOMATIC:  Living expenses up to $2,000.

INTESTATE:  Entire estate if no living issue or parent. Or $50,000 + half of remainder of personal property + real property life estate if living parent or living issue are all surviving spouse's issue. Or half personal property + real property life estate if one or more than one living issue are not issue of surviving spouse.

RIGHT OF ELECTION:  One-third entire estate, adjusted for federal estate tax + transfers. Spouse must elect within six months of personal representative confirmation, or set by court.

# FLORIDA

## Competent Jurisdiction

Circuit Court, state statutes, county by county.

## Last Will and Testament Proving Methods

FORMAL: Testimony of one signing witness, or by personal representative or anyone with knowledge of execution by decedent.

SELF-PROVING: Sanctioned.

## Forms of Administration

SUPERVISED: For all estates.

UNSUPERVISED: Estate with personal property $60,000 or less + all claims discovered + major assets to family members only.

SUMMARY: Allowed where estate does not exceed $25,000 in value.

## Out-of-State Personal Representative, Executor, Executrix

Non-Florida resident allowed if close relative of decedent.

FEES: "Reasonable" fees.

## Court-Appointed Administrator

Court appointed non-Florida okay.

FEES: Same as personal representative.

### Estimated Attorney Fees

"Reasonable" fees. Extraordinary fees okay. Must disclose to heir.

### Asset Inventory and Property Appraisal

Must start within two months of confirmation of personal representative or appointment of administrator. Present to court on demand. Private appraiser at court approval.

### Creditors' Claim Window

Open: three months of first notice.

### Joint Property Ownership

If married, tenants by entirety presumed. Joint tenants must be stated.

### Spousal Shares and Rights

AUTOMATIC: Life estate in real property + personal property up to $11,000 in value. Living expenses during probate up to $6,000.

INTESTATE: Entire estate if no living parent. Or $20,000 + half of remainder if living issue are all surviving spouse's issue. Or half of entire estate if one or more than one living issue are not issue of surviving spouse.

RIGHT OF ELECTION: 30 percent of market value, after debts, of all estate property sited in Florida. Excluded jointly owned savings and trust assets. Spouse must elect within four months of first personal representative notice. If contested and/or litigated = forty days after challenge completion.

## Competent Jurisdiction

Probate Court, state codes, county by county.

## Last Will and Testament Proving Methods

FORMAL:  Testimony of one signing witness.

INFORMAL:  Testimony of one signing witness.

CONTESTED:  Testimony of all signing witnesses or anyone proving signature of decedent.

SELF-PROVING:  No provision for.

## Forms of Administration

SUPERVISED:  For all estates.

SUMMARY:  Allowed where intestate would apply.

## Out-of-State Personal Representative, Executor, Executrix

Non-Georgia resident allowed if bond posted equal to twice estate valuation.

FEES:  2.5 percent of all money + 10 percent of interest on money loaned + 3 percent of property + 10 percent of rental income. Court can provide for higher fees.

## Court-Appointed Administrator

Court-appointed non-Georgia okay if bond posted equal to twice estate valuation.

FEES:  Same as personal representative.

### Estimated Attorney Fees

"Reasonable" fees. Extraordinary fees okay.

### Asset Inventory and Property Appraisal

Must start within four months of confirmation of personal representative or appointment of administrator. Private appraiser okay unless contested.

### Creditors' Claim Window

Open: three months of last notice.

### Joint Property Ownership

Tenants in common assumed. Joint tenants must be stated. No tenants by entirety.

### Spousal Shares and Rights

AUTOMATIC:  Living expenses up to one year.

INTESTATE:  Entire estate if no living parent. Or equal shares with living issue. Or one-quarter of entire estate if four shares.

RIGHT OF ELECTION:  None.

# HAWAII

## Competent Jurisdiction

Circuit Court, state statutes, county by county.

## Last Will and Testament Proving Methods

FORMAL: Testimony of at least one signing witness.

INFORMAL: Testimony or affidavit of anyone with knowledge at decedent's executed will.

CONTESTED: Testimony of at least one signing witness.

SELF-PROVING: Sanctioned.

## Forms of Administration

SUPERVISED: For all estates valued at $40,000 or more or at request of personal representative, executor, executrix, or administrator.

UNSUPERVISED: For estates valued at more than $20,000 but less than $40,000.

SUMMARY: For estates valued at $20,000 or less.

## Out-of-State Personal Representative, Executor, Executrix

Non-Hawaii resident allowed.

FEES: 4 percent of first $15,000 + 3 percent to $85,000 + 2 percent to $900,000 + 1.5 percent to $2,000,000 + 1 percent of all over $2,000,000 + 7 percent of estate income above $5,000. Court can okay higher fees.

## Court-Appointed Administrator

Court appointed non-Hawaii okay.

FEES: Same as personal representative.

## Estimated Attorney Fees

4 percent of first $15,000 + 3 percent to $85,000 + 2 percent to $900,000 + 1.5 percent to $2,000,000 + 1 percent of all over $2,000,000 + other "reasonable" fees. Extraordinary fees okay.

## Asset Inventory and Property Appraisal

Must start within one month of confirmation of personal representative or appointment of administrator or by end of probate. Court will appoint appraiser.

## Creditors' Claim Window

Open: four months of first notice. If no notice = three years. Estate valued at $60,000 or less = two months of first notice.

## Joint Property Ownership

Tenants in common assumed. Joint tenants or tenants by entirety stated.

## Spousal Shares and Rights

AUTOMATIC: Homestead up to $5,000 + $5,000 in personal property + living expenses up to one year.

INTESTATE: Entire estate if no living issue or living parent or half of entire estate.

RIGHT OF ELECTION:   Third of entire estate if owned by deceased since 1977. Must elect within nine months of decedent's death or six months of will proof, whichever is later.

# Idaho

## Competent Jurisdiction

District Court (Magistrate Division), state codes, county by county.

## Last Will and Testament Proving Methods

FORMAL:   Testimony or affidavit of at least one signing witness or other evidence of signing.

INFORMAL:   For estates valued at $40,000 or less = testimony or affidavit of anyone with knowledge of decedent executed will.

CONTESTED:   Testimony of at least one signing witness or other evidence of signing.

SELF-PROVING:   Sanctioned.

## Forms of Administration

SUPERVISED:   Upon petition from interested party. Range of control from full to minimal accounting or as required by court.

SUMMARY:   For estates valued at or less than spouse's automatic share + probate costs + last illness + funeral costs + spouse is sole heir.

## Out-of-State Personal Representative, Executor, Executrix

Non-Idaho resident allowed.

FEES:   "Reasonable" fees. Court can okay higher fees.

### Court-Appointed Administrator

Court appointed non-Idaho okay.

FEES: Same as personal representative.

### Estimated Attorney Fees

"Reasonable" fees. Extraordinary fees okay. Court can okay higher fees.

### Asset Inventory and Property Appraisal

Must start within three months of confirmation of personal representative or appointment of administrator or by end of probate. Private appraiser okay.

### Creditors' Claim Window

Open: four months of first notice. If no notice: three years of decedent's death.

### Joint Property Ownership

Community property in Idaho. Tenants in common assumed. Joint tenants must be stated. No tenants by entirety.

### Spousal Shares and Rights

AUTOMATIC: One-half of community property + homestead from $4,000 to $10,000 + $3,500 in personal property + living expenses up to one year.

INTESTATE: Entire estate if no living issue or living parent. Or $50,000 + half of entire estate if living parent but no living issue or all living issues surviving spouse's.

178

Or half of entire estate if one or more than one issue are not surviving spouse's issue.

RIGHT OF ELECTION: One-half any and all quasi-community property per court guidelines. Must elect within six months of first creditor notice.

# ILLINOIS

## Competent Jurisdiction

Circuit Court, state statutes, county by county.

## Last Will and Testament Proving Methods

FORMAL:   All wills, if contested.

INFORMAL:   Testimony or affidavit of two signing witnesses or anyone with knowledge of handwriting.

SELF-PROVING:   Sanctioned.

## Forms of Administration

SUPERVISED:   Determined by court. Range of control from full to minimal accounting or as required by court.

UNSUPERVISED:   For all estates except where supervised petition accepted by court.

SUMMARY:   If total estate is valued at or below $50,000 + court-imposed guidelines.

AFFIDAVIT:   If total estate, including real property claims, is less than $25,000 after creditor claims and selected costs (funeral).

## Out-of-State Personal Representative, Executor, Executrix

Non-Illinois allowed if named in will and resident agent appointed.

FEES:   "Reasonable" fees.

## Court-Appointed Administrator

Non-Illinois allowed if named in will and resident agent appointed.

FEES:   Same as personal representative.

## Estimated Attorney Fees

"Reasonable" fees.

## Asset Inventory and Property Appraisal

Must start within two months of confirmation of personal representative or appointment of administrator. Private appraiser okay.

## Creditors' Claim Window

Open: six months after notice or appointment of administrator, whichever is later.

## Joint Property Ownership

Tenants in common assumed. Joint tenants must be stated. No tenants by entirety.

## Spousal Shares and Rights

AUTOMATIC:   Family living expenses during probate up to nine months up to $10,000 + $2,000 for each minor issue or handicapped adult issue + homestead valued to $7,500.

INTESTATE:   Entire estate if no living issue. Or half of entire estate if living issue.

RIGHT OF ELECTION:   One-third of estate after debts, if surviving issue. Or half of estate. Must elect within seven months of will proving.

# INDIANA

## Competent Jurisdiction

Circuit Court, Superior Court, Probate Court, state statutes, county by county.

## Last Will and Testament Proving Methods

FORMAL: Testimony or affidavit of at least one signing witness, court can require testimony of two signing witnesses. By court ruling, case by case.

SELF-PROVING: Sanctioned.

## Forms of Administration

SUPERVISED: Imposed by court on a case-by-case basis.

UNSUPERVISED: By agreement of all who could take bylaws of intestacy.

SUMMARY: Not automatic. If less than spouse's automatic share.

AFFIDAVIT: If estate valued at less than $8,500.

## Out-of-State Personal Representative, Executor, Executrix

Non-Indiana resident allowed if bond posted + resident agent appointed.

FEES: "Reasonable" fees.

## Court-Appointed Administrator

Court appointed non-Indiana okay if bond posted + resident agent appointed.

FEES:   Same as personal representative.

### Estimated Attorney Fees

"Reasonable" fees. Extraordinary fees okay.

### Asset Inventory and Property Appraisal

Must start within two months of confirmation of personal representative or appointment of administrator. Private appraiser with court approval.

### Creditors' Claim Window

Open: five months of first creditor notice. Three months if court revokes will.

### Joint Property Ownership

Tenants in common, joint tenants, tenants by entirety okay. If married, tenants by entirety assumed.

### Spousal Shares and Rights

AUTOMATIC:   Personal property up to $8,500 + real estate to make up difference.

INTESTATE:   Entire estate if no living issue or living parent. Or three-quarters of entire estate if living parent but no living issue. Or half of entire estate after creditor claims if one or more than one living issue or living issue of deceased issue. Or life estate in one-third entire estate + intestate share if warranted.

RIGHT OF ELECTION:   One-third personal property after creditor claims + life estate in one-third real property + conditions. Or half entire estate. Spouse must elect within five months of first creditor notice. Or within one month after contested litigation.

# IOWA

## Competent Jurisdiction

District Court, state codes, county by county.

## Last Will and Testament Proving Methods

FORMAL: Testimony or affidavit of one signing witness or testimony of two witnesses establishing handwriting (signature) of deceased and one signing witness.

SELF-PROVING: Sanctioned.

## Forms of Administration

SUPERVISED: For all estates.

SUMMARY: All estates under $50,000 + heir is spouse + no personal representative application.

## Out-of-State Personal Representative, Executor, Executrix

Non-Iowa resident allowed if resident co-personal representative named. Court has ultimate say.

FEES: Set by court. 6 percent on first $1,000 + 4 percent on next $4,000 + 2 percent over $5,000. Court can allow higher fees.

## Court-Appointed Administrator

Court-appointed may be non-Iowa resident if resident co-personal representative named.

FEES: Same as personal representative.

### Estimated Attorney Fees

Same as personal representative. Set by court. Extraordinary fees above court schedule okay.

### Asset Inventory and Property Appraisal

Must start within three months of confirmation of personal representative or appointment of administrator. Appraisal upon request of court or interested party.

### Creditors' Claim Window

Open: four months after second notice of appointment.

### Joint Property Ownership

Tenants in common assumed. Joint tenants must be stated. No tenants by entirety.

### Spousal Shares and Rights

AUTOMATIC: Living expenses up to one year + selected personal property.

INTESTATE: Entire estate if no living issue or all living issue are surviving spouse's. Or entire estate including spouse's automatic share up to $50,000. Or one-half of estate over $50,000 if one or more than one living issue not spouse's.

RIGHT OF ELECTION: One-third of real property + one-third of personal property owned by decedent during marriage + life estate in homestead. Spouse must elect within four months of second creditor notice.

# KANSAS

## Competent Jurisdiction

District Court, state statutes, county by county.

## Last Will and Testament Proving Methods

FORMAL: Testimony or affidavit of two signing witnesses or testimony of anyone establishing handwriting (signature) of deceased.

SELF-PROVING: Sanctioned.

## Forms of Administration

SUPERVISED: For all estates by court dictate or upon request.

UNSUPERVISED: For all other estates.

SUMMARY: All estates under $10,000 + taxes paid + debts paid + no spouse or living issue.

## Out-of-State Personal Representative, Executor, Executrix

Non-Kansas resident allowed if named in will and resident co-personal representative named. Court has final say.

FEES: "Reasonable" fees. Set by court. Court can allow higher fees.

## Court-Appointed Administrator

Court-appointed may be non-Kansas resident if resident co-personal representative named.

FEES:  Same as personal representative.

### Estimated Attorney Fees

"Reasonable" fees. Set by court. Extraordinary fees above court schedule okay.

### Asset Inventory and Property Appraisal

Must start within one month of confirmation of personal representative or appointment of administrator. Court appoints appraiser.

### Creditors' Claim Window

Open: four months after first creditor notice or six months if no supervised probate.

### Joint Property Ownership

Tenants in common assumed. Joint tenants must be stated. No tenants by entirety.

### Spousal Shares and Rights

AUTOMATIC:  All decedent's personal property up to $7,500 in value + life estate in real property.

INTESTATE:  Entire estate if no living issue. Or one-half of entire estate.

RIGHT OF ELECTION:  Intestate share only. Spouse must elect within six months of will proving.

# KENTUCKY

*Competent Jurisdiction*

District Court, state statutes, county by county.

*Last Will and Testament Proving Methods*

FORMAL: Testimony or affidavit of one signing witness or testimony of two witnesses establishing handwriting (signature) of deceased or other evidence.

CONTESTED: Determined by court on a case-by-case basis.

SELF-PROVING: Sanctioned.

*Forms of Administration*

SUPERVISED: For all estates.

SUMMARY: All estates under $5,000 + agreement of intestate parties.

*Out-of-State Personal Representative, Executor, Executrix*

Non-Kentucky resident allowed if related to decedent.

FEES: Set by court. 5 percent on total estate valuation. Court can grant higher fees.

*Court-Appointed Administrator*

Court-appointed may be non-Kentucky resident.

FEES: Same as personal representative.

*Estimated Attorney Fees*

"Reasonable" fees.

## Asset Inventory and Property Appraisal

Must start within two months of confirmation of personal representative or appointment of administrator. Private appraiser okay.

## Creditors' Claim Window

Open: one year of personal representative confirmation or administrator appointment. If no personal representative = three years.

## Joint Property Ownership

If married, tenants in common assumed. Joint tenants must be stated. Tenants by entirety okay.

## Spousal Shares and Rights

AUTOMATIC: One-half all jointly owned property + one-half residential real estate + one-third life estate in all other real property + one-half of all decedent's personal property + living expenses up to $7,500 + last illness and funeral costs.

INTESTATE: Entire estate if no living issue or all living issue, living parents, living siblings, or living issue of siblings. Or same as automatic share.

RIGHT OF ELECTION: Same as automatic share, except one-third of real property limits. Spouse must elect within six months of proving will.

# Louisiana

## Competent Jurisdiction

District Court, state statutes, parish by parish.

## Last Will and Testament Proving Methods

FORMAL: Testimony or affidavit of notary and one signing witness. Or testimony of two signing witnesses. Or testimony of two witnesses establishing handwriting (signature) of deceased or other evidence. Or three signing witnesses.

CONTESTED: Determined by court on a case-by-case basis.

SELF-PROVING: Sanctioned.

## Forms of Administration

SUPERVISED: For all estates. If creditors agree and heirs take liability for decedent's debts, then summary okay.

SUMMARY: All estates under $50,000 + only heir is spouse, decedent's issue, or decedent's siblings.

## Out-of-State Personal Representative, Executor, Executrix

Non-Louisiana resident allowed if resident agent appointed.

FEES: 2.5 percent on all valuation. Court can allow higher fees.

## Court-Appointed Administrator

Court-appointed may be non-Louisiana resident if resident agent appointed.

Fees: Same as personal representative.

*Estimated Attorney Fees*

Open-ended fees.

*Asset Inventory and Property Appraisal*

Upon request by heir. Court appoints three appraisers.

*Creditors' Claim Window*

Open: five years from decedent's death.

*Joint Property Ownership*

Community property in Louisiana. Joint tenants must be stated. No tenants by entirety or tenants in common.

*Spousal Shares and Rights*

Automatic: One-half all community property + one-fourth decedent's share if no issue. Or life estate in one-fourth of entire estate until remarriage if three or less living issue. Or life estate equal to living issue's share if four or more living issue.

Intestate: Entire estate if no living issue or living parents. Or one-half entire estate if no living issue but living parent. Or life estate in entire estate until remarriage.

Right of election: None.

# MAINE

*Competent Jurisdiction*

Probate Court, state statutes, county by county.

*Last Will and Testament Proving Methods*

FORMAL:   Testimony or affidavit of one signing witness.

INFORMAL:   Testimony of anyone establishing handwriting (signature) of deceased.

SELF-PROVING:   Sanctioned.

*Forms of Administration*

SUPERVISED:   Upon petition from interested party. Range of control from full to minimal accounting or as required by court.

UNSUPERVISED:   For all other estates.

SUMMARY:   If estate is less than spouse's automatic share + illness, funeral, and probate costs.

AFFIDAVIT:   All personal property estate under $10,000 in value + thirty-day wait + no personal representative application.

*Out-of-State Personal Representative, Executor, Executrix*

Non-Maine resident allowed.

FEES:   "Reasonable" fees. Court can permit higher fees.

*Court-Appointed Administrator*

Court-appointed may be non-Maine resident.

FEES:   Same as personal representative.

*Estimated Attorney Fees*

"Reasonable" fees. Extraordinary fees okay.

*Asset Inventory and Property Appraisal*

Must start within three months of confirmation of personal representative or appointment of administrator. Private appraiser okay.

*Creditors' Claim Window*

Open: four months after first creditor notice.

*Joint Property Ownership*

Tenants in common assumed. Joint tenants must be stated. No tenants by entirety.

*Spousal Shares and Rights*

AUTOMATIC:   Homestead valued up to $5,000 + personal property valued up to $3,500 + living expenses up to one year.

INTESTATE:   Entire estate if no living issue or living parent. Or $50,000 + half of entire estate if no living issue but living parent or all living issue spouses. Or half of entire estate if one or more than one living issue not surviving spouse's.

RIGHT OF ELECTION:   One-third of entire estate. Spouse must elect within nine months of decedent's death or six months of will proving, whichever is later.

# MARYLAND

## Competent Jurisdiction

Orphan's Court, Circuit Court, state codes, county by county.

## Last Will and Testament Proving Methods

FORMAL: By court order.

INFORMAL: Testimony of anyone with knowledge of decedent's execution.

SELF-PROVING: Sanctioned.

## Forms of Administration

SUPERVISED: For all estates.

SUMMARY: All estates under $20,000.

## Out-of-State Personal Representative, Executor, Executrix

Non-Maryland resident allowed if resident agent appointed.

FEES: Set by court. 10 percent on first $20,000 + 4 percent over $20,000 + 10 percent on real property.

## Court-Appointed Administrator

Court-appointed may be non-Maryland resident if resident agent appointed.

FEES: Same as personal representative.

### Estimated Attorney Fees

"Reasonable" fees. Extraordinary fees above court schedule okay.

### Asset Inventory and Property Appraisal

Must start within three months of confirmation of personal representative or appointment of administrator. Court-appointed appraiser.

### Creditors' Claim Window

Open: six months after personal representative appointment + extensions available.

### Joint Property Ownership

If married, tenants by entirety assumed. Joint tenants must be stated. Tenants in common okay.

### Spousal Shares and Rights

AUTOMATIC:  Living expenses up to $2,000 + $1,000 for each minor living issue.

INTESTATE:  Entire estate if no living parent or living issue. Or one-half of estate if living issue is a minor (eighteen). Or $15,000 + one-half entire estate if issue is age of majority (eighteen) or parent is living but no living issue.

RIGHT OF ELECTION:  One-third of entire estate after all debts paid if living issue. Or one-half of entire estate. Spouse must elect within one month of creditor filing deadline.

# MASSACHUSETTS

## Competent Jurisdiction

District Court (Probate and Family Divisions), state laws, county by county.

## Last Will and Testament Proving Methods

FORMAL: Testimony or affidavit of one signing witness.

SELF-PROVING: Sanctioned.

## Forms of Administration

SUPERVISED: For all estates.

SUMMARY: If estate is comprised of only personal property valued at less than $15,000 + wait thirty days + no personal representative application.

## Out-of-State Personal Representative, Executor, Executrix

Non-Massachusetts allowed if resident agent also appointed.

FEES: Open-ended fees.

## Court-Appointed Administrator

Court-appointed non-Massachusetts allowed if resident agent also appointed.

FEES: Same as personal representative.

## Estimated Attorney Fees

Open-ended fees.

## Asset Inventory and Property Appraisal

Must start within three months of confirmation of personal representative or appointment of administrator. Private appraiser okay.

## Creditors' Claim Window

Open: four months after personal representative posts bond.

## Joint Property Ownership

Joint tenants, tenants in common, and tenants by entirety okay. If married, tenants by entirety assumed.

## Spousal Shares and Rights

AUTOMATIC: Living expenses + use of home for up to six months. May qualify for homestead up to $100,000.

INTESTATE: Entire estate if no living parent, living issue, living siblings, living first cousins or their living issue. Or entire estate if valued at less than $200,000 + one-half of remainder if no living issue but other living relative. Or one-half of estate if one or more than one living issue.

RIGHT OF ELECTION: One-third estate if living issue. Or $25,000 + one-half of personal property + one-half real property held in life estate if no living issue but living relatives. Or $25,000 + one-half entire estate if no living relatives, or life estate in one-third real property. Spouse must elect within six months after will proving.

# MICHIGAN

## Competent Jurisdiction

Probate Court, state statutes, county by county.

## Last Will and Testament Proving Methods

FORMAL: Testimony or affidavit of one signing witness or by proof of handwriting of decedent and witnesses.

INFORMAL: Valid if will contains statutory signatures.

SELF-PROVING: Sanctioned.

## Forms of Administration

SUPERVISED: Upon petition from any interested party. Range of control from full to minimal accounting or as required by court.

UNSUPERVISED: For all other estates.

SUMMARY: If estate is less than spouse's automatic share + illness, funeral, and probate costs.

AFFIDAVIT: If estate is comprised of personal property valued under $5,000.

## Out-of-State Personal Representative, Executor, Executrix

Non-Michigan allowed.

FEES: "Reasonable" fees.

## Court-Appointed Administrator

Court-appointed non-Michigan allowed.

FEES: Same as personal representative.

### Estimated Attorney Fees

"Reasonable" fees.

### Asset Inventory and Property Appraisal

Must start within two to three months of confirmation of personal representative or appointment of administrator. Private appraiser okay.

### Creditors' Claim Window

Open: two to four months after creditor notice. If no notice, three years from death date.

### Joint Property Ownership

Joint tenants, tenants in common, and tenants by entirety okay. Joint tenants must be stated. If married, tenants by entirety assumed.

### Spousal Shares and Rights

AUTOMATIC: Homestead up to $10,000 + personal property up to $3,500 + living expenses during probate up to one year.

INTESTATE: Entire estate if no living parent or living issue. Or $60,000 + one-half of entire estate if living parent but no living issue or all living issue are all surviving spouse's issue. Or one-half of entire estate if one or more than one living issue are not surviving spouse's.

RIGHT OF ELECTION: One-half entire estate. Or life estate in one-third real property acquired during marriage. Spouse must elect within two months of creditor claims or inventory deadline, whichever is later.

# MINNESOTA

## Competent Jurisdiction

Probate Court, County Court, state statutes, county by county.

## Last Will and Testament Proving Methods

FORMAL: Testimony of one signing witness.

INFORMAL: Testimony or affidavit from anyone with knowledge of decedent's execution.

CONTESTED: Testimony of one signing witness.

SELF-PROVING: Sanctioned.

## Forms of Administration

SUPERVISED: Upon petition from interested party. Range of control from full to minimal accounting or as required by court.

UNSUPERVISED: For all estates except where supervised petition accepted by court.

SUMMARY: If total estate, excluding real property claims, is less than spouse's marital exemption added to administration, last illness, and funeral costs.

AFFIDAVIT: If total estate, including real property claims, is less than $5,000 + thirty-day wait + no pending personal representative application.

## Out-of-State Personal Representative, Executor, Executrix

Non-Minnesota resident allowed.

FEES: "Reasonable" fees.

### Court-Appointed Administrator

Court may appoint non-Minnesota resident.

FEES:  Same as personal representative.

### Estimated Attorney Fees

"Reasonable" fees. Extraordinary fees okay.

### Asset Inventory and Property Appraisal

Must start within six months of confirmation of personal representative or appointment of administrator. Or nine months from decedent's death. Private appraiser at court approval.

### Creditors' Claim Window

Open: four months after first notice.

### Joint Property Ownership

Tenants in common assumed. Joint tenants must be stated. No tenants by entirety.

### Spousal Shares and Rights

AUTOMATIC:  Personal property valued up to $9,000 + one car + living expenses up to eighteen months + life estate in homestead if living issue.

INTESTATE:  Entire estate if no living parent or living issue. Or $7,000 + one-half of estate if living issue are all surviving spouse's. Or one-half entire estate if one or more than one living issue not surviving spouse's.

RIGHT OF ELECTION:  One-third of entire estate. Spouse must elect within nine months of death or six months after will proving, whichever is later.

# MISSISSIPPI

## Competent Jurisdiction

Chancery Court, state codes, county by county.

## Last Will and Testament Proving Methods

FORMAL: Testimony of one signing witness. Or testimony or affidavit from anyone with knowledge of decedent's execution.

SELF-PROVING: Sanctioned.

## Forms of Administration

SUPERVISED: For all estates.

AFFIDAVIT: If total estate is less than $10,000 + thirty-day wait + no pending personal representative application.

## Out-of-State Personal Representative, Executor, Executrix

Non-Mississippi resident allowed.

FEES: 7 percent of entire estate. Extraordinary fees above court schedule okay.

## Court-Appointed Administrator

Court may appoint non-Mississippi resident.

FEES: Same as personal representative.

## Estimated Attorney Fees

"Reasonable" fees. Extraordinary fees okay.

### Asset Inventory and Property Appraisal

Must start within three months of confirmation of personal representative or appointment of administrator. Court appoints appraiser.

### Creditors' Claim Window

Open: three months after first notice.

### Joint Property Ownership

Joint tenants, tenants in common, and tenants by entirety okay. Tenants in common assumed. Joint tenants must be stated.

### Spousal Shares and Rights

AUTOMATIC: Life estate in homestead valued to $30,000 + living expenses for up to one year.

INTESTATE: Entire estate if no living issue. Or equal share with all living issue.

RIGHT OF ELECTION: One-half of entire estate if no issue. Or one-third of entire estate if any issue. Or zero if estate equals intestate share. Spouse must elect within three months of will proving.

# Missouri

## Competent Jurisdiction

Circuit Court (Probate Division), state statutes, county by county.

## Last Will and Testament Proving Methods

FORMAL:  Testimony of two signing witnesses.

INFORMAL:  Testimony of one signing witness and proof of signature.

SELF-PROVING:  Sanctioned.

## Forms of Administration

SUPERVISED:  Upon petition from interested party. Range of control from full to minimal accounting or as required by court.

UNSUPERVISED:  For all estates except where supervised petition accepted by court.

SUMMARY:  If total estate's value is less than spouse's share + if spouse applies. Or if estate is valued at less than $5,000 and creditor petitions court. Or if estate is valued at less than $15,000 + thirty-day wait + no pending personal representative application.

## Out-of-State Personal Representative, Executor, Executrix

Non-Missouri resident allowed if resident agent appointed.

FEES:  5 percent of first $5,000 + 4 percent of next $20,000 + 3 percent of next $75,000 + 2.75 percent of next \$300,000 + 2.5 percent of next \$600,000 + 2 percent over \$1,000,000. Court can provide for higher fees.

### Court-Appointed Administrator

Court may appoint non-Missouri resident if resident agent appointed.

FEES:   Same as personal representative.

### Estimated Attorney Fees

Same as personal representative. Extraordinary fees above court schedule okay.

### Asset Inventory and Property Appraisal

Must start within one month of confirmation of personal representative or appointment of administrator. Private appraiser at court approval.

### Creditors' Claim Window

Open: six months after first notice. If no notice, then three years from date of decedent's death.

### Joint Property Ownership

Joint tenants, tenants in common, and tenants by entirety okay. Tenants in common assumed. Joint tenants must be stated.

### Spousal Shares and Rights

AUTOMATIC:   Selected personal property + "reasonable" living expenses up to one year + life estate in homestead up to one-half estate value or $7,500, whichever is less.

INTESTATE: Entire estate if no living parent or living issue. Or $20,000 + one-half of estate if no living issue or all living issue are surviving spouse's. Or one-half entire estate if one or more than one living issue not surviving spouse's.

RIGHT OF ELECTION: One-third of entire estate if no issue. Or one-third of entire estate. Spouse must elect within six months after first creditor notice.

# MONTANA

## Competent Jurisdiction

District Court, state codes, county by county.

## Last Will and Testament Proving Methods

FORMAL: Testimony of one signing witness.

INFORMAL: Testimony of anyone with proof of signature.

SELF-PROVING: Sanctioned.

## Forms of Administration

SUPERVISED: Upon petition from interested party. Range of control from full to minimal accounting or as required by court.

UNSUPERVISED: For all estates except where supervised petition accepted by court.

SUMMARY: If total estate, after debts, is valued at less then $7,500 + thirty-day wait + no pending personal representative.

## Out-of-State Personal Representative, Executor, Executrix

Non-Montana resident allowed.

FEES: "Reasonable" fees up to 3 percent of first $40,000 + 2 percent of amount over $40,000. Court can provide for higher fees.

### Court-Appointed Administrator

Court may appoint non-Montana resident if resident agent appointed.

FEES:  Same as personal representative.

### Estimated Attorney Fees

One and one-half times rate of personal representative, court can provide for higher. Extraordinary fees above court schedule okay.

### Asset Inventory and Property Appraisal

Must start within three months of confirmation of personal representative or appointment of administrator. Private appraiser at court approval.

### Creditors' Claim Window

Open: four months after first notice. If no notice, then three years from date of decedent's death.

### Joint Property Ownership

"Partnership interests," joint tenants, tenants in common okay. Tenants in common assumed. Joint tenants must be stated.

### Spousal Shares and Rights

AUTOMATIC:  Homestead value up to $20,000 + personal property valued up to $3,500 + living expenses up to one year.

INTESTATE:  Entire estate if no living parent or living issue or all issue are surviving spouse's. Or one-half entire estate if one living issue not surviving spouse's. Or one-third of entire estate if more than one living issue not surviving spouse's.

RIGHT OF ELECTION:   One-third of entire estate. Spouse must elect within nine months after decedent's death.

# Nebraska

## Competent Jurisdiction

County Court, state statutes, county by county.

## Last Will and Testament Proving Methods

FORMAL: Testimony or affidavit of one signing witness.

INFORMAL: Testimony or affidavit of anyone with knowledge of decedent's execution.

CONTESTED: Testimony of one signing witness.

SELF-PROVING: Sanctioned.

## Forms of Administration

SUPERVISED: Upon petition from interested party. Range of control from full to minimal accounting or as required by court.

UNSUPERVISED: For all estates except where supervised petition accepted by court.

SUMMARY: If total estate, minus real estate, is valued at less than last illness, funeral, allowances, and probate costs.

AFFIDAVIT: If total estate is valued at less than $10,000 + thirty-day wait + no pending personal representative application.

## Out-of-State Personal Representative, Executor, Executrix

Non-Nebraska resident allowed.

Fees: "Reasonable" fees. Court can provide for higher fees.

## Court-Appointed Administrator

Court may appoint non-Nebraska resident.

Fees: Same as personal representative.

## Estimated Attorney Fees

"Reasonable" fees. Court can provide for higher. Extraordinary fees okay.

## Asset Inventory and Property Appraisal

Must start within two months of confirmation of personal representative or appointment of administrator. Private appraiser at court approval.

## Creditors' Claim Window

Open: two months after first creditor notice. If no notice, then three years from date of decedent's death.

## Joint Property Ownership

Joint tenants and tenants in common okay. Joint tenants must be stated. No tenants of entirety.

## Spousal Shares and Rights

Automatic: Homestead value up to $7,500 + personal property valued up to $5,000 + living expenses up to one year.

Intestate: Entire estate if no living parent or living issue. Or $50,000 + one-half entire estate if living parent but no living issue. Or one-half of entire estate if one or more than one living issue not surviving spouse's.

RIGHT OF ELECTION: One-half of entire estate. Spouse must elect within nine months after decedent's death or six months from proving will, whichever is later.

# NEVADA

## Competent Jurisdiction

District Court, state statutes, county by county.

## Last Will and Testament Proving Methods

FORMAL:   Testimony or affidavit of one signing witness.

SELF-PROVING:   Sanctioned.

## Forms of Administration

SUPERVISED:   For all estates.

SUMMARY:   If total estate is valued at less than $100,000. Court permission required.

AFFIDAVIT:   If total estate is valued at less than $10,000 + no real estate + forty-day wait + no pending personal representative application.

## Out-of-State Personal Representative, Executor, Executrix

Non-Nevada resident not allowed.

FEES:   4 percent of first $15,000 + 3 percent of next $85,000 + 2 percent amount over $85,000. Court can provide for higher fees.

## Court-Appointed Administrator

Court will not appoint non-Nevada resident.

FEES:   Same as personal representative.

### Estimated Attorney Fees

"Reasonable" fees. Court can provide for higher. Extraordinary fees above court schedule okay.

### Asset Inventory and Property Appraisal

Must start within two months of confirmation of personal representative or appointment of administrator. Private appraiser at court approval.

### Creditors' Claim Window

Open: three months after first notice. If no notice, then two months before final accounting.

### Joint Property Ownership

Community property in Nevada. Joint tenants and tenants in common okay. Joint tenants must be stated. No tenants by entirety.

### Spousal Shares and Rights

AUTOMATIC: One-half community property + personal property by court approval + living expenses determined by court.

INTESTATE: Entire separate property of decedent if no issue, living siblings, living issue of issue, or living parent. Or one-half separate estate if one living issue or living issue of issue, living sibling, or living parent. Or one-third separate property if more than one living issue or one living issue and living issue of deceased or living issue of deceased issue.

RIGHT OF ELECTION: None.

# NEW HAMPSHIRE

*Competent Jurisdiction*

Probate Court, state statutes, county by county.

*Last Will and Testament Proving Methods*

FORMAL:   Testimony of two signing witness.

INFORMAL:   Testimony of one signing witness.

SELF-PROVING:   Sanctioned.

*Forms of Administration*

SUPERVISED:   For all estates.

SUMMARY:   If total estate is valued at less than $5,000.

*Out-of-State Personal Representative, Executor, Executrix*

Non–New Hampshire resident allowed if resident agent appointed.

FEES:   Open-ended fees.

*Court-Appointed Administrator*

Court may appoint non–New Hampshire resident if resident agent appointed.

FEES:   Same as personal representative.

*Estimated Attorney Fees*

Open-ended fees.

### Asset Inventory and Property Appraisal

Must start within three months of confirmation of personal representative or appointment of administrator. Court will appoint three appraisers.

### Creditors' Claim Window

Open: six months after appointment of personal representative.

### Joint Property Ownership

Tenants in common assumed. Joint tenants must be stated. If married = joint tenants. No tenants of entirety.

### Spousal Shares and Rights

AUTOMATIC: Use of home and living expenses for forty days. Living expenses during probate are deducted from share.

INTESTATE: Entire estate if no living parent or living issue. Or $50,000 + one-half entire estate if living parent but no living issue. Or one-half of entire estate if one or more than one living issue not surviving spouse's.

RIGHT OF ELECTION: One-third of entire estate if any living issue. Or $10,000 value in personal property + $10,000 value in real property + one-half of remainder if no living issue. Or $10,000 + $2,000 for each year of marriage + one-half of remainder of estate if no living issue, living parents, or living siblings. Spouse must elect within six months after appointment of personal representative.

# NEW JERSEY

## Competent Jurisdiction

Surrogate Court, Superior Court, state statutes, county by county.

## Last Will and Testament Proving Methods

FORMAL: Testimony of at least one signing witness, but court can require two.

INFORMAL: Testimony or affidavit of anyone with knowledge of decedent's execution.

CONTESTED: Testimony of one signing witness.

SELF-PROVING: Sanctioned.

## Forms of Administration

SUPERVISED: Upon petition from interested party. Range of control from full to minimal accounting or as required by court.

UNSUPERVISED: For all estates except where supervised petition accepted by court.

AFFIDAVIT: If total estate is valued at less than $10,000 + thirty-day wait + no pending personal representative application.

## Out-of-State Personal Representative, Executor, Executrix

Non–New Jersey resident allowed if bond posted.

FEES: 6 percent. Court can provide for higher fees.

### Court-Appointed Administrator

Court may appoint non–New Jersey resident if bond posted.

FEES: Same as personal representative.

### Estimated Attorney Fees

"Reasonable" fees. Court can provide for higher. Extraordinary fees above court schedule okay.

### Asset Inventory and Property Appraisal

Must start within three months of confirmation of personal representative or appointment of administrator. Private appraiser at court approval.

### Creditors' Claim Window

Open: six months after first creditor notice.

### Joint Property Ownership

Tenants in common, joint tenants, or tenants by entirety okay. If married, tenants by entirety assumed.

### Spousal Shares and Rights

AUTOMATIC: Living expenses during probate. Not automatic.

INTESTATE: Entire estate if no living parent or living issue. Or $50,000 + one-half entire estate if living parent but no living issue. Or one-half of entire estate if one or more than one living issue not surviving spouse's.

RIGHT OF ELECTION:   One-third of entire estate. Or life estate in one-half of real property acquired during marriage. Spouse must elect within six months from appointment of personal representative.

# NEW MEXICO

## Competent Jurisdiction

District Court, Probate Court, state statutes, county by county.

## Last Will and Testament Proving Methods

FORMAL: Testimony or affidavit of one signing witness.

INFORMAL: Testimony or affidavit of anyone with knowledge of decedent's execution.

CONTESTED: Testimony of one signing witness or other evidence.

SELF-PROVING: Sanctioned.

## Forms of Administration

SUPERVISED: Upon petition from interested party. Range of control from full to minimal accounting or as required by court.

UNSUPERVISED: For all estates except where supervised petition accepted by court.

SUMMARY: If estate is valued at less than last illness and funeral costs, probate fees, and spouse's share.

AFFIDAVIT: If total estate is valued at less than $20,000 + thirty-day wait + no pending personal representative application.

## Out-of-State Personal Representative, Executor, Executrix

Non–New Mexico resident allowed.

Fees:  10 percent of first \$30,000 + 5 percent of balance, with some exceptions. Court can provide for higher fees.

### Court-Appointed Administrator

Court may appoint non–New Mexico resident.

Fees:  Same as personal representative.

### Estimated Attorney Fees

Same as personal representative fees. Court can provide for higher. Extraordinary fees above court schedule okay.

### Asset Inventory and Property Appraisal

Must start within three months of confirmation of personal representative or appointment of administrator. Private appraiser at court approval.

### Creditors' Claim Window

Open: two months after first creditor notice. If no notice, then three years from decedent's death.

### Joint Property Ownership

Community property in New Mexico. Community property, tenants in common, and joint tenants okay. No tenants by entirety.

### Spousal Shares and Rights

Automatic:  One-half community property + personal property up to \$3,500 in value + living expenses up to $10,000. Court may award homestead up to $100,000.

INTESTATE: Entire estate if no living issue. Or one-fourth separate property + decedent's community property.

RIGHT OF ELECTION: None.

# NEW YORK

## Competent Jurisdiction

Surrogate's Court, state laws, county by county.

## Last Will and Testament Proving Methods

UNCONTESTED:   Testimony or affidavit of at least one signing witness.

CONTESTED:   Testimony of one signing witness, or verification of signature.

SELF-PROVING:   Sanctioned.

## Forms of Administration

SUPERVISED:   Upon petition from interested party. Range of control from full to minimal accounting or as required by court.

UNSUPERVISED:   For all estates except where supervised petition accepted by court.

SUMMARY:   If total estate is valued at less than $10,000 in personal property if spouse applies. If no spouse, next heir.

AFFIDAVIT:   If total estate is valued at less than $10,000 + thirty-day wait + all debts paid.

## Out-of-State Personal Representative, Executor, Executrix

Non–New York resident allowed.

FEES:   5 percent of first $100,000 + 4 percent of next $200,000 + 3 percent of next $700,000 + 2.5 percent of next $4,000,000 + 2 percent on balance. Court can provide for higher fees.

### Court-Appointed Administrator

Court may appoint non–New York resident.

FEES:   Same as personal representative.

### Estimated Attorney Fees

"Reasonable" fees. Court can provide for higher. Extraordinary fees above court schedule okay.

### Asset Inventory and Property Appraisal

Must start within six months of proving will. Private appraiser at court approval.

### Creditors' Claim Window

Open: three months after first creditor notice. If no notice, seven months from approval of personal representative.

### Joint Property Ownership

Tenants in common, joint tenants, or tenants by entirety okay. If married, tenants by entirety assumed.

### Spousal Shares and Rights

AUTOMATIC:   Household items valued up to $5,000 + farm equipment up to $100,000 + all other personal property up to $1,000.

INTESTATE:   Entire estate if no living parent or living issue. Or $25,000 + one-half entire estate if living parent but no living issue. Or $4,000 + one-half of entire estate if only one. Or $4,000 + one-third of entire estate if more than one living issue.

RIGHT OF ELECTION:   One-half of entire estate if living issue. Or one-third of entire estate. Spouse must elect within six months from appointment of personal representative.

# NORTH CAROLINA

## Competent Jurisdiction

Superior Court, state statutes, county by county.

## Last Will and Testament Proving Methods

FORMAL:  Testimony of two signing witnesses, or one witness + other evidence.

INFORMAL:  Testimony of any interested party with a rightful claim.

SELF-PROVING:  Sanctioned.

## Forms of Administration

SUPERVISED:  For all estates.

AFFIDAVIT:  If total estate is valued at less than $10,000 + thirty-day wait.

## Out-of-State Personal Representative, Executor, Executrix

Non–North Carolina resident allowed if resident agent appointed.

FEES:  5 percent. Court clerk will set fees and can provide for higher fees.

## Court-Appointed Administrator

Court may appoint non–North Carolina resident if resident agent appointed.

FEES:  Same as personal representative.

### Estimated Attorney Fees

"Reasonable" fees. Court can provide for higher. Extraordinary fees above court schedule okay.

### Asset Inventory and Property Appraisal

Must start within three months of confirmation of personal representative or appointment of administrator. Private appraiser at court approval.

### Creditors' Claim Window

Open: six months after first creditor notice.

### Joint Property Ownership

Tenants in common, joint tenants, or tenants by entirety okay.

### Spousal Shares and Rights

AUTOMATIC: Living expenses per formula set by court during probate. Not automatic.

INTESTATE: Entire estate if no living parent or living issue. Or $15,000 worth of personal property + one-half entire estate if living issue. Or $15,000 worth of personal property + one-third of entire estate if two or more living issue. Or $25,000 worth of personal property + one-half entire estate if no living issue but living parent. Different proportions may apply.

RIGHT OF ELECTION: Life estate in home. Or one-third of all real property acquired during marriage. Spouse must elect within thirteen months of all claim filing limits.

# North Dakota

## Competent Jurisdiction

District Court, state codes, county by county.

## Last Will and Testament Proving Methods

FORMAL: Testimony of one signing witness, or other evidence.

INFORMAL: Testimony or affidavit of anyone with knowledge of decedent's execution.

CONTESTED: Testimony of one signing witness, or other evidence.

SELF-PROVING: Sanctioned.

## Forms of Administration

SUPERVISED: Upon petition from interested party. Range of control from full to minimal accounting or as required by court.

UNSUPERVISED: For all estates except where supervised petition accepted by court.

SUMMARY: If estate, less real property, is less than value of homestead + spouse's share + last illness + funeral + probate costs.

AFFIDAVIT: If total estate is valued at less than $15,000 + thirty-day wait + no pending personal representative application.

## Out-of-State Personal Representative, Executor, Executrix

Non–North Dakota resident allowed.

FEES: "Reasonable" fees.

## Court-Appointed Administrator

Court may appoint non–North Dakota resident.

FEES: Same as personal representative.

## Estimated Attorney Fees

"Reasonable" fees. Court can provide for higher. Extraordinary fees above court schedule okay.

## Asset Inventory and Property Appraisal

Must start within six months of confirmation of personal representative or appointment of administrator or nine months after death of decedent. Private appraiser at court approval.

## Creditors' Claim Window

Open: three months after first creditor notice. If no notice, three years from date of death of decedent.

## Joint Property Ownership

Tenants in common or joint tenants okay. No tenants by entirety.

## Spousal Shares and Rights

AUTOMATIC: Life estate in home and land + $5,000 worth of personal property + living expenses up to one year.

INTESTATE: Entire estate if no living parent or living issue. Or $50,000 + one-half entire estate if living parent but no living issue or if living issue are surviving spouse's. Or one-half of entire estate if one or more than one living issue not surviving spouse's.

RIGHT OF ELECTION:    One-third of entire estate. Spouse must elect within six months from proving will or nine months from death of decedent.

# OHIO

*Competent Jurisdiction*

Common Pleas Court (Probate Division), state codes, county by county.

*Last Will and Testament Proving Methods*

FORMAL: Testimony or affidavit of two execution witnesses, or other evidence.

SELF-PROVING: Sanctioned.

*Forms of Administration*

SUPERVISED: For all estates.

SUMMARY: If estate, less real property, is less than value of homestead + spouse's share + last illness + funeral + probate costs.

AFFIDAVIT: If total estate is valued at less than $25,000.

*Out-of-State Personal Representative, Executor, Executrix*

Non-Ohio resident allowed if named in will and relative of decedent.

FEES: 4 percent of first $100,000 + 3 percent of next $300,000 + 2 percent of balance + 1 percent of all nonprobate property used to calculate Ohio estate taxes. Court can provide for higher fees.

*Court-Appointed Administrator*

Court may appoint non-Ohio resident.

FEES: Same as personal representative.

### Estimated Attorney Fees

Case by case. Set by court.

### Asset Inventory and Property Appraisal

Must start within one month of confirmation of personal representative or appointment of administrator. Private appraiser at court approval.

### Creditors' Claim Window

Open: three months after first creditor notice.

### Joint Property Ownership

Tenants in common or tenants by entirety, with exceptions, okay. Joint tenants must be stated.

### Spousal Shares and Rights

AUTOMATIC: One-year use of home + living expenses up to $5,000, deducted from share.

INTESTATE: Entire estate if no living issue. Or $60,000 + half entire estate if only one living issue. Or $60,000 + one-third of entire estate if two or more living issue. Or $20,000 + half of entire estate if one living issue not surviving spouse's. Or $20,000 + one-third of entire estate if two living issue or more than two living issue not surviving spouse's.

RIGHT OF ELECTION: Half of entire estate if one living issue. Or one-third of entire estate. Spouse must elect within one month from notice or three months from any will contest.

# OKLAHOMA

## Competent Jurisdiction

District Court, state statutes, county by county.

## Last Will and Testament Proving Methods

FORMAL:   Testimony of one signing witness.

CONTESTED:   Testimony of all signing witnesses, or other evidence.

SELF-PROVING:   Sanctioned.

## Forms of Administration

SUPERVISED:   For all estates.

SUMMARY:   For estates less than $60,000.

## Out-of-State Personal Representative, Executor, Executrix

Non-Oklahoma resident allowed, if resident agent appointed.

FEES:   5 percent of first $1,000 + 4 percent of next $4,000 + 2.5 percent of balance.

## Court-Appointed Administrator

Court may appoint non-Oklahoma resident, if resident agent appointed.

FEES:   Same as personal representative.

## Estimated Attorney Fees

"Reasonable" fees. Extraordinary fees above court schedule okay.

## Asset Inventory and Property Appraisal

Must start within two months of confirmation of personal representative or appointment of administrator or nine months after death of decedent. Court may appoint appraiser.

## Creditors' Claim Window

Open: one to two months after first creditor notice, with exceptions.

## Joint Property Ownership

Tenants in common, joint tenants, and tenants by entirety okay. Joint tenants must be stated.

## Spousal Shares and Rights

AUTOMATIC: Life estate in home + selected personal property + living expenses up to one year. Not automatic.

INTESTATE: Entire estate if no living parent, living sibling, or living issue. Or all jointly acquired estate + half remainder of entire estate if no living issue but living parent or living sibling. Or half entire estate if all living issue are surviving spouse's. Or half of all jointly acquired estate if one or more than one living issue not surviving spouse's + another equal share with issue.

RIGHT OF ELECTION: Half of all jointly acquired property. Spouse must elect by date of distribution.

# Oregon

## Competent Jurisdiction

Circuit Court, state statutes, county by county.

## Last Will and Testament Proving Methods

FORMAL: Testimony of one signing witness.

CONTESTED: Testimony of one signing witness, or knowledge of validity of signatures.

SELF-PROVING: Sanctioned.

## Forms of Administration

SUPERVISED: For all estates.

UNSUPERVISED: For all estates except where supervised petition accepted by court.

SUMMARY: If estate is necessary for support and maintenance of surviving spouse and living issue. Case-by-case basis.

AFFIDAVIT: If total estate is comprised of personal property and valued at less than $35,000 + thirty-day wait.

## Out-of-State Personal Representative, Executor, Executrix

Non-Oregon resident allowed.

FEES: 7 percent of first $1,000 + 4 percent of next $9,000 + 3 percent of next $40,000 + 2 percent of higher + 1 percent of qualifying Oregon property. Court can provide for higher fees.

### Court-Appointed Administrator

Court may appoint non-Oregon resident.

FEES:   Same as personal representative.

### Estimated Attorney Fees

"Reasonable" fees. Court can provide for higher fees. Extraordinary fees above court schedule okay.

### Asset Inventory and Property Appraisal

Must start within two months of confirmation of personal representative or appointment of administrator. Private appraiser at court approval.

### Creditors' Claim Window

Open: twelve months after first creditor notice or final accounting, whichever is earlier. If no notice, three years from date of death of decedent.

### Joint Property Ownership

Tenants in common or tenants by entirety okay. Joint tenants must be stated.

### Spousal Shares and Rights

AUTOMATIC:   Use of home for one year + living expenses up to two years. Not automatic.

INTESTATE:   Entire estate after debts paid if no living issue or all living issue are surviving spouse's. Or half of entire estate after debts paid if one or more than one living issue not surviving spouse's.

RIGHT OF ELECTION: One-quarter of entire estate. Spouse must elect within three months from proving will or one month from inventory filing, whichever is later.

# PENNSYLVANIA

### Competent Jurisdiction

Court of Common Pleas (Orphan's Court Division), Registrar of Wills, state codes, county by county.

### Last Will and Testament Proving Methods

FORMAL:   Testimony of two signing witnesses, or competent person, or signature proof.

SELF-PROVING:   Sanctioned.

### Forms of Administration

SUPERVISED:   For all estates.

UNSUPERVISED:   If intestacy would apply.

AFFIDAVIT:   If total estate is comprised of real property + personal property valued at less than $10,000.

### Out-of-State Personal Representative, Executor, Executrix

Non-Pennsylvania resident allowed with approval of registrar.

FEES:   "Reasonable" fees.

### Court-Appointed Administrator

Court may appoint non-Pennsylvania resident.

FEES:   Same as personal representative.

### Estimated Attorney Fees

"Reasonable" fees. Court can provide for higher. Extraordinary fees okay.

### Asset Inventory and Property Appraisal

Must start within nine months after death of decedent. Private appraiser at court approval.

### Creditors' Claim Window

Open: twelve months from date of death of decedent.

### Joint Property Ownership

Tenants in common and tenants by entirety okay. Joint tenants must be stated. If married, tenants by entirety assumed.

### Spousal Shares and Rights

AUTOMATIC: Living expenses up to $2,000.

INTESTATE: Entire estate if no living parent or living issue. Or $30,000 + one-half entire estate if living parent but no living issue or if living issue are surviving spouse's. Or one-half of entire estate if one or more than one living issue not surviving spouse's.

RIGHT OF ELECTION: One-third of entire estate. Spouse must elect within six months from proving will.

# Rhode Island

## Competent Jurisdiction

Probate Court, state laws, county by county.

## Last Will and Testament Proving Methods

FORMAL: Testimony of two signing witnesses, or testimony of two persons with ability to prove signature, or other evidence.

SELF-PROVING: No.

## Forms of Administration

SUPERVISED: For all estates.

SUMMARY: If estate is less than spouse's automatic share + illness, funeral, and probate debts.

AFFIDAVIT: All personal property estate under $10,000 in value + forty-five-day wait + no personal representative application.

## Out-of-State Personal Representative, Executor, Executrix

Non–Rhode Island resident allowed on case-by-case basis.

FEES: "Reasonable" fees. Court can allow higher fees.

## Court-Appointed Administrator

Court-appointed may be non–Rhode Island resident on case-by-case basis.

FEES: Same as personal representative.

### Estimated Attorney Fees

"Reasonable" fees. Extraordinary fees okay.

### Asset Inventory and Property Appraisal

Must start within one month of confirmation of personal representative or appointment of administrator. Private appraiser okay with court approval. Exceptions.

### Creditors' Claim Window

Open: for six months after notice.

### Joint Property Ownership

Tenants in common assumed. Joint tenants must be stated. Tenants by entirety okay.

### Spousal Shares and Rights

AUTOMATIC:  Selected personal property + living expenses up to six months.

INTESTATE:  $75,000 worth of real property + life estate in balance of real property. Or $50,000 in personal property + one-half entire estate if no living issue. Or one-half personal property.

RIGHT OF ELECTION:  Life estate in real property. Spouse must elect within six months of will proving.

# South Carolina

## Competent Jurisdiction

Probate Court, state codes, county by county.

## Last Will and Testament Proving Methods

FORMAL: Testimony or affidavit of one signing witness, or other evidence.

INFORMAL: Testimony of anyone establishing handwriting (signature) of deceased.

CONTESTED: Testimony of at least one signing witness.

SELF-PROVING: Sanctioned.

## Forms of Administration

SUPERVISED: For all estates.

SUMMARY: If intestate estate is valued at less than $10,000 after certain debts and costs deducted.

AFFIDAVIT: For estates under $10,000 in value + thirty-day wait + no personal representative application.

## Out-of-State Personal Representative, Executor, Executrix

Non–South Carolina resident allowed.

FEES: 5 percent of value of estate. Court can allow higher fees.

## Court-Appointed Administrator

Court-appointed may be non–South Carolina resident.

FEES:   Same as personal representative.

## Estimated Attorney Fees

"Reasonable" fees. Extraordinary fees above court schedule okay.

## Asset Inventory and Property Appraisal

Must start within two months of confirmation of personal representative or appointment of administrator. Court-appointed appraiser.

## Creditors' Claim Window

Open: eight months after first notice.

## Joint Property Ownership

Tenants in common assumed. Joint tenants must be stated. No tenants by entirety.

## Spousal Shares and Rights

AUTOMATIC:   Selected personal property + $5,000.

INTESTATE:   Entire estate if no living issue. Or one-half entire estate if one or more than one living issue.

RIGHT OF ELECTION:   One-third entire estate. Spouse must elect within eight months of decedent's death.

# SOUTH DAKOTA

## Competent Jurisdiction

Circuit Court, state laws, county by county.

## Last Will and Testament Proving Methods

UNCONTESTED:   None, if mailing requirements met.

CONTESTED:   Testimony of all signing witnesses or by proof of decedent's handwriting.

SELF-PROVING:   Sanctioned.

## Forms of Administration

SUPERVISED:   Upon petition from interested party. Range of control from full to minimal accounting or as required by court.

UNSUPERVISED:   For all estates except where supervised petition accepted by court.

SUMMARY:   If estate is less than $60,000 in value.

AFFIDAVIT:   All personal property estate under $5,000 in value + thirty-day wait + no personal representative application.

## Out-of-State Personal Representative, Executor, Executrix

Non–South Dakota allowed if resident agent appointed.

FEES:   5 percent of first $1,000 + 4 percent of next $4,000 + 2.5 percent all above. Court can provide for higher fees.

### Court-Appointed Administrator

Court-appointed non–South Dakota allowed if resident agent appointed.

FEES:   Same as personal representative.

### Estimated Attorney Fees

Open-ended fees.

### Asset Inventory and Property Appraisal

Must start within nine months of decedent's death. Private appraiser okay.

### Creditors' Claim Window

Open: two months after creditor notice.

### Joint Property Ownership

Joint tenants and tenants in common okay. Joint tenants must be stated. No tenants by entirety.

### Spousal Shares and Rights

AUTOMATIC:   Life estate in homestead + personal property up to $1,500 + living expenses during probate up to one year.

INTESTATE:   Entire estate if no living parent, living siblings, or living issue. Or one-half of entire estate only one living issue or issue of deceased issue. Or one-third of entire estate if two living issue or two living issue of deceased issue. Or $100,000 + one-half of entire estate if no living issue but living parent, living sibling, or sibling's issue.

RIGHT OF ELECTION: $100,000 or one-third of entire estate, whichever is greater. Spouse must elect within six months from decedent's death or before final distribution order, whichever is earlier.

# TENNESSEE

## Competent Jurisdiction

Chancery Court, Probate Court, state codes, county by county.

## Last Will and Testament Proving Methods

FORMAL: Testimony of all signing witnesses or by proof of decedent's handwriting.

INFORMAL: Testimony or affidavit of at least one signing witness.

SELF-PROVING: No.

## Forms of Administration

SUPERVISED: For all estates.

SUMMARY: If entire estate is comprised of only personal property less than $10,000 in value + forty-five-day wait + no personal representative application.

## Out-of-State Personal Representative, Executor, Executrix

Non-Tennessee allowed if resident co-personal representative also appointed.

FEES: "Reasonable" fees.

## Court-Appointed Administrator

Court-appointed non-Tennessee allowed if resident co-personal representative also appointed.

FEES: Same as personal representative.

*Estimated Attorney Fees*

"Reasonable" fees.

*Asset Inventory and Property Appraisal*

Must start within two months of confirmation of personal representative or appointment of administrator. Private appraiser okay.

*Creditors' Claim Window*

Open: six months after creditor notice.

*Joint Property Ownership*

Tenants by entirety and tenants in common okay. Joint tenants must be stated.

*Spousal Shares and Rights*

AUTOMATIC: Life estate in homestead to value of $5,000 + living expenses during probate up to one year. Court sets amount on a case-by-case basis.

INTESTATE: Entire estate if no living issue. Or one-third of entire estate or living issue share, whichever is greater.

RIGHT OF ELECTION: One-third net (after debts) entire estate. Spouse must elect within nine months from decedent's death or six months after confirmation of personal representative or appointment of administrator.

# TEXAS

## Competent Jurisdiction

Statutory Probate Court, state statutes, county by county.

## Last Will and Testament Proving Methods

FORMAL: Testimony or affidavit of one signing witness, or other proof of handwriting.

SELF-PROVING: Sanctioned.

## Forms of Administration

SUPERVISED: Upon petition from interested party. Range of control from full to minimal accounting or as required by court.

UNSUPERVISED: For all estates by intestate or contest.

SUMMARY: For estates valued at or less than spouse's living expenses. Or entire estate comprised only of personal property valued at less than $50,000. Or if heir posts bond two times entire estate's appraised value.

## Out-of-State Personal Representative, Executor, Executrix

Non-Texas resident allowed if resident agent also appointed.

FEES: 5 percent of most assets. Court can approve higher fees.

## Court-Appointed Administrator

Court-appointed non-Texas resident allowed if resident agent also appointed.

FEES:   Same as personal representative.

### Estimated Attorney Fees

"Reasonable" fees. Extraordinary fees okay. Court can approve higher fees.

### Asset Inventory and Property Appraisal

Must start within three months of confirmation of personal representative.

### Creditors' Claim Window

Open: six months of confirmation of personal representative or appointment of administrator.

### Joint Property Ownership

Community property in Texas. Tenants in common okay. Joint tenants must be stated. No tenants by entirety.

### Spousal Shares and Rights

AUTOMATIC:   One-half of community property + $1,000 of value in personal property + living expenses up to one year + life estate in home, at court's choice.

INTESTATE:   Entire community property estate if no living issue. Or one-half of entire community property estate if living issue.

RIGHT OF ELECTION:   None.

# UTAH

## Competent Jurisdiction

District Court, state codes, county by county.

## Last Will and Testament Proving Methods

FORMAL:   Testimony or affidavit of one signing witness, or other evidence.

INFORMAL:   Testimony or affidavit from anyone with knowledge of decedent's execution.

CONTESTED:   Testimony of at least one signing witness, or other evidence.

SELF-PROVING:   Sanctioned.

## Forms of Administration

SUPERVISED: Upon petition from interested party. Range of control from full to minimal accounting or as required by court.

UNSUPERVISED:   For all estates except where supervised petition accepted by court.

SUMMARY: If total estate, excluding real property claims, is less than spouse's marital exemption + homestead value + last illness + administration + funeral costs.

AFFIDAVIT: If total estate, excluding real property claims, is less than $25,000 + thirty-day wait + no pending personal representative application.

### Out-of-State Personal Representative, Executor, Executrix

Non-Utah resident allowed.

FEES: "Reasonable" fees.

### Court-Appointed Administrator

Court may appoint non-Utah resident.

FEES: Same as personal representative.

### Estimated Attorney Fees

"Reasonable" fees. Extraordinary fees above court schedule okay.

### Asset Inventory and Property Appraisal

Must start within three months of confirmation of personal representative or appointment of administrator. Private appraiser at court approval.

### Creditors' Claim Window

Open: three months after first notice. If no notice, within three years of decedent's death.

### Joint Property Ownership

Tenants in common, joint tenants, and tenants by entirety okay. Joint tenants must be stated.

### Spousal Shares and Rights

AUTOMATIC: Selected personal property valued up to $5,000 + cars valued up to $25,000 + living expenses up to twelve months + home valued up to $10,000.

INTESTATE:   Entire estate if no living parent or living issue. Or one-half of estate if one or more than one living issue not surviving spouse's.

RIGHT OF ELECTION:   One-third of entire estate. Spouse must elect within twelve months of decedent's death or six months after will proving, whichever is later. Exemptions apply.

# VERMONT

## Competent Jurisdiction

Probate Court, state statutes, county by county.

## Last Will and Testament Proving Methods

FORMAL:   Testimony of one signing witness, or other evidence.

SELF-PROVING:   No provision.

## Forms of Administration

SUPERVISED:   For all estates.

SUMMARY:   If total estate is comprised of only personal property valued at $10,000 or less.

## Out-of-State Personal Representative, Executor, Executrix

Non-Vermont resident allowed on case-by-case basis.

FEES:   "Necessary" fees.

## Court-Appointed Administrator

Court may appoint non–Vermont resident on case-by-case basis.

FEES:   Same as personal representative.

## Estimated Attorney Fees

Open-ended fees.

### Asset Inventory and Property Appraisal

Must start within one month of confirmation of personal representative or appointment of administrator. Private appraiser at court approval.

### Creditors' Claim Window

Open: four months after first notice. If no notice, within three years of decedent's death.

### Joint Property Ownership

Tenants in common, joint tenants, and tenants by entirety okay. Joint tenants must be stated.

### Spousal Shares and Rights

AUTOMATIC: Living expenses up to eight months + homestead valued up to $30,000.

INTESTATE: Entire estate if no living issue or other living relative. Or $25,000 + one-half of entire estate if no living issue. Or one-third of all personal property + one-half of all real property if one living issue is also surviving spouse's. Or one-third of all personal property + one-third of all real estate if two or more than two living issue or one or more than one living issue not surviving spouse's.

RIGHT OF ELECTION: One-half of entire estate, after debts, if only one living issue and issue is surviving spouse's. Spouse must elect within eight months of will proving.

# VIRGINIA

## Competent Jurisdiction

Circuit Court, state codes, county by county.

## Last Will and Testament Proving Methods

FORMAL:   Testimony of all possible heirs.

INFORMAL: Testimony or affidavit of one signing witness or from anyone with knowledge of witnesses' signature.

SELF-PROVING:   Sanctioned.

## Forms of Administration

SUPERVISED:   For all estates.

AFFIDAVIT:   If total estate is less than $5,000 + sixty-day wait + no pending personal representative application.

## Out-of-State Personal Representative, Executor, Executrix

Non-Virginia resident not allowed unless sole heir and resident agent appointed.

FEES:   "Reasonable" fees.

## Court-Appointed Administrator

Court will not appoint non-Virginia resident unless sole heir and resident agent appointed.

FEES:   Same as personal representative.

## Estimated Attorney Fees

Open-ended fees.

## Asset Inventory and Property Appraisal

Must start within four months of confirmation of personal representative or appointment of administrator. Private appraiser at court approval + court review of final statement.

## Creditors' Claim Window

Open: twelve months after notice. Court can add six months.

## Joint Property Ownership

Tenants in common, joint tenants, and tenants by entirety okay. Joint tenants must be stated.

## Spousal Shares and Rights

AUTOMATIC: Selected personal property valued up to $3,500 + living expenses up to twelve months + home valued to $5,000 (deducted from share).

INTESTATE: Entire estate if no living issue. Or one-third of estate if one or more than one living issue not surviving spouse's.

RIGHT OF ELECTION: One-third of entire estate if living issue. Or one-half entire estate if no living issue. Spouse must elect within twelve months of will proving.

# WASHINGTON

## Competent Jurisdiction

Superior Court (Probate Division), state codes, county by county.

## Last Will and Testament Proving Methods

FORMAL: Testimony of two signing witnesses, or other evidence (handwriting).

SELF-PROVING: No provision.

## Forms of Administration

SUPERVISED: If requested in will or upon petition from interested party. Range of control from full to minimal accounting or as required by court.

UNSUPERVISED: For all estates except where supervised petition accepted by court and personal representative not an heir.

AFFIDAVIT: If total estate is less than $30,000 + forty-day wait + no pending personal representative application.

## Out-of-State Personal Representative, Executor, Executrix

Non-Washington resident allowed if resident agent also appointed.

FEES: "Reasonable" fees.

## Court-Appointed Administrator

Court may appoint non-Washington resident if resident agent also appointed.

FEES:    Same as personal representative.

### Estimated Attorney Fees

"Reasonable" fees. Extraordinary fees okay.

### Asset Inventory and Property Appraisal

Must start within three months of confirmation of personal representative or appointment of administrator. Private appraiser at court approval.

### Creditors' Claim Window

Open: four months after first notice or filing with clerk.

### Joint Property Ownership

Community property in Washington. Tenants in common and joint tenants okay. Joint tenants must be stated. No tenants by entirety.

### Spousal Shares and Rights

AUTOMATIC:    One-half community property + "reasonable" family expenses + other at court's choice.

INTESTATE:    All community property estate if no living issue or living parent. Or one-half of all community property + three-fourth separate property estate if no living issue but living parent or living sibling. Or all community property estate + one-half separate property estate if living issue.

RIGHT OF ELECTION:    None.

# WEST VIRGINIA

## Competent Jurisdiction

County Commission, state codes, county by county.

## Last Will and Testament Proving Methods

FORMAL: Testimony of all signing witnesses, verified signature or other evidence.

SELF-PROVING: Sanctioned.

## Forms of Administration

SUPERVISED: For all estates.

SUMMARY: For estates with only one heir. Or if total estate is valued at less than $50,000; $100,000 in certain counties.

## Out-of-State Personal Representative, Executor, Executrix

Non–West Virginia resident allowed only if specific relationship to decedent + county commissioner appointed agent + bond posted.

FEES: "Reasonable" fees.

## Court-Appointed Administrator

Court may appoint non–West Virginia resident only if specific relationship to decedent + county commissioner appointed agent + bond posted.

FEES: Same as personal representative.

## Estimated Attorney Fees

"Reasonable" fees. Extraordinary fees okay.

## Asset Inventory and Property Appraisal

Must start within eight months of confirmation of personal representative or appointment of administrator. Commissioner will appoint three to five appraisers.

## Creditors' Claim Window

Open: two to three months after first notice.

## Joint Property Ownership

Tenants in common, joint tenants, and tenants by entirety okay. Joint tenants must be stated.

## Spousal Shares and Rights

AUTOMATIC:   Selected personal property valued up to $1,000 + use of home until minor issue attains age twenty-one. Or dower share.

INTESTATE:   Entire estate if no living issue. Or one-third of estate if one or more than one living issue.

RIGHT OF ELECTION:   One-third of entire estate. Or one-third life estate of one-third real property dower. Spouse must elect within eight months of proving will or if will contest two months after ruling.

# WISCONSIN

## Competent Jurisdiction

Circuit Court, state statutes, county by county.

## Last Will and Testament Proving Methods

INFORMAL: None if properly executed and witnessed.

CONTESTED: Testimony or affidavit of one signing witness, or other evidence.

SELF-PROVING: No provision.

## Forms of Administration

SUPERVISED: Upon petition from interested party. Range of control from full to minimal accounting or as required by court.

UNSUPERVISED: For all estates except where supervised petition accepted by court.

SUMMARY: If total estate is less than $10,000 in value.

AFFIDAVIT: If total estate is less than $5,000.

## Out-of-State Personal Representative, Executor, Executrix

Non-Wisconsin resident allowed if resident agent also appointed.

FEES: 2 percent. Court can provide for higher fees.

## Court-Appointed Administrator

Court may appoint non-Wisconsin resident if resident agent also appointed.

FEES:    Same as personal representative.

## Estimated Attorney Fees

"Reasonable" fees. Extraordinary fees okay.

## Asset Inventory and Property Appraisal

Must start within six months of confirmation of personal representative or appointment of administrator. Private appraiser at court approval + court may review statement.

## Creditors' Claim Window

Open: three months after court order.

## Joint Property Ownership

Tenants in common and joint tenants okay. If married, joint tenants assumed. No tenants by entirety.

## Spousal Shares and Rights

AUTOMATIC:    One-half of qualifying property + personal property up to $1,000 (not automatic) + living expenses during probate + life estate or ownership of home valued to $10,000 or less.

INTESTATE:    Entire estate if no living issue or all issue surviving spouse's. Or one-half of estate if one or more than one living issue not surviving spouse's.

RIGHT OF ELECTION:    None.

# WYOMING

### Competent Jurisdiction

District Court, state statutes, county by county.

### Last Will and Testament Proving Methods

FORMAL: Testimony or affidavit of one signing witness, or other evidence.

SELF-PROVING: No provision for.

### Forms of Administration

SUPERVISED: For all estates.

UNSUPERVISED: For all estates except where supervised petition accepted by court.

AFFIDAVIT: If total estate is less than $30,000 + thirty-day wait + no pending personal representative application.

### Out-of-State Personal Representative, Executor, Executrix

Non-Wyoming resident allowed if resident co-personal representative also named.

FEES: 10 percent of first $1,000 + 5 percent of next $4,000 + 3 percent of next $15,000 + 2 percent of balance. Court can approve more.

### Court-Appointed Administrator

Court may appoint non-Wyoming resident if resident co-personal representative also named.

FEES:   Same as personal representative.

*Estimated Attorney Fees*

Same as personal representative. Court can approve more. Extraordinary fees above court schedule okay.

*Asset Inventory and Property Appraisal*

Must start within four months of initial filing. Private appraiser okay.

*Creditors' Claim Window*

Open: three months after creditor notice.

*Joint Property Ownership*

Tenants in common, joint tenants, and tenants by entirety okay. Joint tenants must be stated.

*Spousal Shares and Rights*

AUTOMATIC:   Use of home and clothing until filing of inventory + "reasonable" living expenses (not automatic) + home valued up to $30,000 (case by case).

INTESTATE:   Entire estate if no living issue. Or one-half of estate if one or more than one living issue.

RIGHT OF ELECTION:   One-half of entire estate if no living issue or living issue are all surviving spouse's. Or one-fourth entire estate if one living issue or more than one living issue are not surviving spouse's. Spouse must elect within three months after will proving or one month from filing whichever is later.

# Appendix II:
# Executor, Executrix, Personal Representative, or Administrator Checklist

There are many tasks and functions that must be performed by an executor, executrix, personal representative, or administrator to settle an estate before the probate court. These functions must be completed in a systematic order as directed by probate laws, statutes, codes, and the court in the state of residence of the decedent and any other state where the decedent owned property.

In order to help you through this process and keep track of where you are, where you have been, and where you are going next, I have provided the following checklist. If you are an heir of an estate, you can use this list to keep tabs on the attorney and/or executor, executrix, personal representative, or administrator who may have been selected to settle the estate.

Because of the particular needs or scope of the probate settlement being managed, all of the following items may or may not be needed in your settlement process.

___ Find the last will and testament of the decedent.
___ Read the last will and testament.

___ Start organizing system.

___ Contact all "interested parties" and heirs.

___ Contact decedent's employer. Collect wages, salary, and benefits.

___ Contact credit card companies, utilities, landlord, and post office.

___ Consult with attorney who drew up the decedent's last will and testament.

___ Contact Social Security and other government agencies.

___ Collect veteran and surviving spouse death benefits.

___ Examine all books, accounts, and files.

___ Begin information-gathering on decedent-owned business.

___ Notify banks, safe deposit, thrift companies, and other financial institutions.

___ Review insurance policies.

___ Contact insurance companies.

___ Get SS4 form from IRS (1-800-555-1212) and apply for estate tax ID number.

___ Present the last will and testament to the probate court for proving.

___ Get notarized witness affidavits, if needed.

___ Discuss right of election with surviving spouse.

___ If the decedent left no last will and testament, file proper intestate form(s).

___ If last will and testament is lost, file proper loss and will form(s).

___ Apply to the court for confirmation as executor, executrix, personal representative, or administrator.

___ Apply for court orders of estate administration.

___ File oath and pay for bond.

— If last will and testament is contested, acquire evidence and witness declarations.
— Receive letters of administration or letters testamentary.
— Notify creditors by mail, in person, or publication.
— Depending on the estate, select the method of probate, if possible.
— Account for items found in safe deposit box.
— Secure tax waivers.
— Open estate checking account at local bank.
— Make claims for money due estate.
— Take control of any and all assets owed the estate.
— Inventory and appraise personal property.
— Arrange for supervision and management of business.
— Take custody of securities.
— Collect dividends, interest or payments. Provide for the management of stock and bond investments.
— Review condition, leases, taxes, and mortgages on real estate.
— Arrange for the management and/or maintenance of real property.
— Set aside and hold nonprobate property and/or asset.
— Begin ancillary probate in other state where property was owned by decedent.
— Hire private or court-appointed appraiser(s).
— Appraise all property as of date of death or six months from that date.
— Deliver inventory and appraised value of estate to court.
— Deliver inventory and appraised value of estate to all heirs.

- Administer the estate as dictated by the decedent's last will and testament, estate needs, and/or court requirements.
- Review all personal property marketability for potential court-ordered sale.
- Review all real estate marketability for potential court-ordered sale.
- Review business and business property marketability for potential court-ordered sale.
- Review all securities marketability for potential court-ordered sale.
- Review all other forms of assets and/or property marketability for potential court-ordered sale.
- Sell assets to pay taxes.
- Prepare and pay decedent's final income tax returns within nine months of his or her passing.
- Prepare and pay state of residence estate tax.
- Prepare and pay ancillary state estate tax.
- Prepare and pay federal inheritance tax.
- Prepare and pay state of residence inheritance tax.
- Prepare and pay ancillary state inheritance tax.
- Release securities and property in other states.
- Review claims filed against the estate.
- Calculate claim balances and cash needs.
- Sell assets to pay claims.
- Pay lawyer, administrator, executor, executrix, or personal representative fees.
- Pay all approved claims.
- Prepare and deliver to court final estate accounting.
- Make special distributions and bequests as directed in last will and testament.

\_\_ Make distributions to heirs and get receipts for same.

\_\_ Close estate.

\_\_ Obtain your final discharge as executor, executrix, personal representative, or administrator.

\_\_ Deliver probate files to court.

\_\_ Keep copies of all documents for the statutory period of time dictated by the court(s).

# Appendix III: Surviving or Successor Trustee Checklist

There are many tasks and functions that must be performed by a surviving spouse who is a trustee or the successor trustee(s) to settle an estate held in a living trust. These tasks and functions should be done in a systematic order.

In order to help you through this process and keep track of where you are, where you have been, and where you are going next, I have provided the following checklist. If you are a primary beneficiary of a trust estate, you can use this list to keep informed about the process as the successor trustee goes about the duties of settling this estate.

Because of the particular needs or scope of the trust estate settlement being managed, all of the following items may or may not be needed.

__ Find the living trust document and pore over the will.

__ Read trust document.

__ Start organizing system.

__ Contact all "interested parties" and heirs.

__ Contact decedent's employer. Collect wages, salary, and benefits.

__ Contact credit card companies, utilities, landlord, and post office.

___ Consult with estate planner or attorney who drew up the decedent's trust document.
___ Contact Social Security and other government agencies.
___ Collect veteran and surviving spouse death benefits.
___ Examine all books, accounts, and files.
___ Begin information-gathering on decedent-owned business.
___ Notify banks, safe deposit, thrift companies, and other financial institutions.
___ Review insurance policies.
___ Contact insurance companies.
___ Get SS4 form from IRS (1-800-555-1212) and apply for estate tax ID number.
___ If trust is contested (very rare), acquire evidence.
___ Notify creditors by mail, in person.
___ Open trust estate checking account at local bank.
___ Make claims for money due estate.
___ Take control of any and all assets owed the estate.
___ Arrange for supervision and management of business.
___ Take custody of securities.
___ Collect dividends, interest, or payments. Provide for the management of stock and bond investments.
___ Review condition, leases, taxes, and mortgages on real estate.
___ Arrange for the management and/or maintenance of real property.
___ Hire private appraiser.
___ Appraise all property as of date of death or six months from that date.
___ Divide trust into A, B, and/or C portions.

— Manage the estate as dictated by the decedent's trust and estate needs.
— Review all personal property, real estate, business, securities, and all other forms of assets and/or property marketability.
— Place assets into A, B, and/or C portions.
— Sell assets to pay taxes.
— Prepare and pay decedent's final income tax returns within nine months of his or her passing.
— Prepare and pay state of residence estate tax.
— Prepare and pay ancillary state estate tax.
— Prepare and pay federal inheritance tax.
— Prepare and pay state of residence inheritance tax.
— Prepare and pay ancillary state inheritance tax.
— Calculate claim balances and cash needs.
— Sell assets to pay claims.
— Pay all approved claims.
— Make special distributions and bequests as directed in trust or memorandum.
— Make distributions to heirs and get receipts for same.

# One Final Thought on Trust Settlement

If you are settling an estate through a trust, you are embarking on an experience that should be very rewarding. I have helped many clients plan their estates so that their surviving spouse and children will not have to go through the agony and expense of probate.

Do you need a living trust?

The time for proper estate planning is when you are alive. Consider all your hard work and plan for its transfer to your loved ones upon your death.

The time to plan your estate is *now*.

To learn more about how to protect your family and estate from probate and unnecessary taxes, read the Hastings House book *The Living Trust Simplified*, by Stephen C. Brecht, available at bookstores nationwide.

To those requiring special assistance in estate planning or the various trusts, please direct correspondence to:

Estate Planning Services
20555 Dumont Street
Woodland Hills, CA 91364
(818) 888-1057
"The Living Trust Specialists"

# Index

Beneficiary *(Cont.)*
  intestate succession and decease
    of, 24–25
  joint tenant ownership and, 13–
    14
  of last will and testament, 13–
    14, 19–21, 24–25, 58–59
  of living trust, 87, 95
  as minor, 79, 89–90, 114–15
  notification of death sent to, 53–
    54, 58–59
Beneficiary change, survivor's
    trust A and, 127
Bequests, *see* Special bequests
Bond, posting, 61
Bonds, joint tenant ownership
    and, 12
  *see also* Securities
Borrowing, trustee having power
    regarding, 112–14
Brokerage houses, notification of
    death sent to, 53–54
Broker, *see* Real estate broker
Budget Reconciliation Act of 1993,
    142
Burger, Warren, 26–27
Business
  closing, 65–66
  selling, 65
  supervision and management of
    ongoing, 65–66
Business agreements, in estate
    settlement organizer, 48
Business associates, notification of
    death sent to, 53–54, 58–
    59
Business broker, 65
Business cards, in estate
    settlement organizer, 48
Business insurance, estate
    settlement and, 51
Business interests of decedent,
    acquiring knowledge of, 52–
    53
Business taxes, 74
Bypass trust, *see* A-B married
    revocable living trust

Capital gains tax, sale of securities
    and, 67

Capital gains taxes, 144
  joint tenant ownership and, 15–
    18
Cash, collecting for probate, 63
Charity, living trust and, 100–101
Children, last will and testament
    naming, 44
Claims
  probate and, 75–76, *see also*
    Creditors
  trustee having power over, 121–
    22
Clemens, Samuel Langhorne, 56
CMA, *see* Comparative market
    analysis
Coadministrators, intestate
    succession and, 23
Codicils
  to last will and testament, 38
  petition for probate needing, 57
Commonly owned property,
    income tax liability and, 18–19
Common probate, *see*
    Unsupervised probate
Community property, income tax
    liability and, 18–19
Comparative market analysis
    (CMA), real estate broker
    providing, 68
Conservator, incapacitated joint
    tenant designating, 15
"Contested claim," probate and, 64
Corporation, decedent's business
    as, 53
Cost basis, capital gain and, 15–18
Creditors, 54
  joint tenancy and, 14
  notification of death sent to, 53–
    54, 58–59
  probate and, 64–65, 75–76
Credit unions, notification of
    death sent to, 53–54

Death certificate(s)
  certified copies of, 46
  insurance claims needing, 49
  number of copies needed of, 63
  petition for probate needing, 57
Decedent's trust B, 129–33
Decedent's trust C, 133–37

278

280

282